Harmony of Faith and Science

By

Tracy Leclear

As

'The Heavenly Hippie'

12808 West Airport Blvd Suite 270M Sugar Land, TX 77478,
Unites States

https://www.theempirepublishers.com/

Our books may be purchased in bulk for promotional, educational, or business use.

Please contact The Empire Publishers at +1 844 636-4579, or by email at support@theempirepublishers.com

First Edition August 2025

About the Author

Tracy LeClear is a soul-awakened seeker who walks the edge where science meets spirit, weaving divine truth into every step of her journey.

Dedication

To my son, the light that led me back to truth when the
world went dim.

To my grandmother, whose quiet strength taught me that
faith is a living act of love, not just a practice.

And to every soul who has walked with me, whether through
lesson or blessing, you are a part of this becoming.

Acknowledgements

To God, my constant, my redeemer, my source.

Without You, this book would not exist. Every word, every revelation, every divine alignment belongs to You.

To my son, your wisdom, even in your youth, has been a light in my darkest hours and a reminder of what unconditional love looks like.

This journey, this awakening, is for you, and because of you.

To my grandmother, your unwavering faith and grace in living out your beliefs taught me that spirituality transcends religion.

You planted seeds in me that would later bloom into awakening. I carry your strength within me always.

To those who challenged me, loved me, broke me, and walked with me, you shaped the path beneath my feet.

You were each a part of the alchemy that turned confusion into clarity, and fear into faith.

To the scientists, spiritual teachers, and mystics, past and present, who stood at the threshold of mystery and dared to ask the hard questions.

You inspired me to believe that truth needs no defense, only the courage to be seen.

To my readers, thank you for opening this book with an open mind and heart.

May it awaken something ancient within you.

To my ancestors and spiritual guides, your presence has been felt through dreams, symbols, and the quiet wisdom that has guided my pen.

And finally, to the woman I used to be and the one I am still becoming, thank you for never giving up on the deeper knowing, and for finally allowing your voice to rise.

Table of Contents

Introduction

This book was born not from ambition, but from awe. It was a quiet, reverent awe that grew in my heart each time my son spoke to me of the stars.

He was just a child then, wide-eyed and curious, his small hands wrapped around books thicker than his wrists. While other children played, he read about galaxies and gravity, black holes and atomic bonds. He spoke of the constellations with the same reverence some reserve for scripture, and in those moments, he became my teacher.

Through his eyes, science was no longer something to fear, it became something sacred. It didn't draw me away from God. It brought me closer. It was as though, in understanding how the universe works, I began to understand the mind of the One who made it.

It was my son who taught me this: to love God, I must first be unafraid to look at His creation. To worship Him fully, I must be willing to study the world He so carefully and wondrously designed.

In our modern age, many stand at the fork in the road where science and faith appear to part ways. They believe to walk one path is to abandon the other. Science, they say, is for the rational; faith, for the blind. One seeks truth by reason, the other clings to belief without proof. And yet, how tragic this false divide.

Because truth, in its purest form, does not conflict with itself.

Science and faith are not adversaries. They are partners in the pursuit of understanding. They are two voices in a symphony, each echoing the other, pointing to something greater than themselves. Where science asks *how*, faith asks *why*. And in their union, we glimpse the fullness of meaning.

This book is an offering, a quiet invitation to see what I have come to see: that the truths uncovered by science are not threats to belief but reflections of the very God we worship. The universe, in all its order and complexity, testifies to a mind beyond comprehension and a love beyond measure.

The Bible was never meant to be a science textbook. Yet its pages are filled with truth that resonates with the discoveries of modern science. It speaks of light before the sun, of order before chaos, of purpose behind design. And when we read Scripture with open hearts and scientific minds, we begin to see something beautiful, that faith is not afraid of knowledge. It welcomes it.

Consider the great thinkers of the past: Isaac Newton, Johannes Kepler, James Clerk Maxwell. These men were not threatened by science; they were inspired by it. Their work was not a rebellion against God, but a devotion to Him. They studied the laws of nature not to disprove the divine, but to uncover it. They saw the fingerprints of the Creator in every equation, every orbit, every atom.

In the chapters ahead, we will explore the sacred harmony between Scripture and science. Together we'll examine:

- The mathematical elegance that holds the cosmos in perfect balance, a reflection of divine order.

- The elemental building blocks of life, each one a testament to thoughtful design.

- The subatomic particles, invisible to the naked eye, through which God upholds the very fabric of the universe.

- The laws of gravity, motion, and thermodynamics. constant, unwavering, mirroring the steadfastness of our Creator.

- Prophetic truths written in ancient texts that science has only recently begun to confirm.

We will also face the misunderstandings, the doubts, the arguments that have long driven a wedge between belief and reason. But we will do so gently, not to win debates, but to heal division. And perhaps, if we're willing, we'll come to see that science does not diminish God. It magnifies Him.

For every law discovered, every element named, every mystery solved, none of it explains away the divine. Instead, it reveals a God who is not only present, but purposeful. Not only powerful, but precise. A God who writes in particles and poetry, in DNA and Psalms, in galaxies and Genesis.

This journey is for the questioning heart and the curious mind. For the scientist who kneels in wonder, and the believer who gazes at the stars. It is for those who have ever wondered if faith can survive in the age of reason, and for those who suspect it may thrive.

May you find in these pages not only knowledge, but worship. Not only answers, but awe.

For when we seek truth, truly seek it, we find God already waiting there.

And through it all, I return to the boy who first opened my eyes, the one whose wonder became my own. This book is for him, whose love for the stars helped me see the face of God in all things.

Chapter 1
Mathematics is the Language of Creation

I. Introduction

"Mathematics is the language in which God has written the universe."

—*Galileo Galilei*

At first glance, the worlds of Christianity and mathematics might appear to be orbiting in entirely different galaxies. One speaks the language of faith, miracles, and mystery; the other, the language of reason, logic, and proof. The one kneels at the altar of the unseen; the other stands firmly on the ground of the provable. Can belief in divine mystery coexist with a discipline so firmly rooted in precision?

For centuries, people have wrestled with this apparent contradiction. Faith is often dismissed as irrational or anti-intellectual, a matter of blind trust. Mathematics, meanwhile, is portrayed as the height of human reason, entirely separate from the heart or soul. Some claim that to be religious is to abandon critical thinking, while others suggest that mathematical thinking leaves no room for spiritual belief.

But such a division is not only false, it is deeply misleading. At its heart, Christianity is not a rejection of reason, but a pursuit of truth. Similarly, mathematics is not merely the manipulation of numbers, but a language for understanding the deep structure of the universe. Both disciplines ask profound questions: *What is true? What is real? What is eternal?*

Both the mathematician and the believer are seekers. The Christian seeks the mind and heart of God; the mathematician seeks the patterns and principles that govern the created world. These are not conflicting quests, they are parallel paths, sometimes intersecting, always pointing beyond the visible toward a deeper order.

5

In this chapter, we will explore how Christianity and mathematics are not adversaries, but allies, each reflecting the fingerprints of a Creator who values truth, order, and beauty. Far from being opposites, faith and logic may, in fact, be part of the same divine equation.

II. God as the Author of Order and Structure

The Christian faith begins not in randomness or chaos, but in structure, rhythm, and intentional design. *"In the beginning, God created the heavens and the earth"* (Genesis 1:1). These ten words set the stage for everything that follows, not only in Scripture but in the inherent reality. The God of Christianity is not a distant, disinterested force but an intentional Creator whose fingerprints are embedded in the laws that govern the universe. At every level, from the cosmic to the cellular, there is a discernible structure, one that reflects both mathematical precision and divine intentionality.

To understand God as the Author of order is to see beyond the superficial split between science and religion, logic and faith, reason and revelation. In the Christian worldview, the existence of logical laws and consistent patterns in the universe is not a coincidence but a reflection of God's nature.

The Bible consistently presents God as a being who brings structure out of chaos. The creation narrative in Genesis 1 is perhaps the most striking illustration of this divine ordering process. The earth initially is described as "formless and empty," with darkness over the surface of the deep (Genesis 1:2). But then, God speaks. Through a sequence of intentional acts, He brings light, separates waters, gathers land, places celestial bodies, populates the skies and seas, and eventually breathes life into humanity. Each stage of creation is marked by order and rhythm, culminating with the declaration: *"God saw all that He had made, and it was very good."* (Genesis 1:31).

This passage is more than poetic theology; it is an affirmation of design and structure. Each day of creation corresponds to the next in a symmetry that almost mirrors a mathematical grid:

Day	Act of Forming	Day	Act of Filling
1	Light & Darkness	4	Sun, Moon, Stars
2	Sky & Waters	5	Birds & Sea Creatures
3	Land & Vegetation	6	Land Animals & Humans

God creates habitats and then fills them in a mirrored pattern. This logical framework is not accidental. Instead, it is deeply purposeful. It suggests that order is not merely a human concept but a divine principle.

The idea of God as a bringer of order recurs throughout Scripture. In the book of Job, when Job dares to question the justice of his suffering, God responds not with sentiment but with a litany of rhetorical questions that underscore the mathematical and structural grandeur of the cosmos:

"Where were you when I laid the earth's foundation? Tell me, if you understand. Who marked off its dimensions? Surely you know!" (Job 38:4–5)

This passage, filled with architectural and numerical language, foundations, measurements, boundaries, reminds the reader that creation is not haphazard. It is built with care, with a plan, and with knowledge beyond human comprehension.

Moreover, Paul affirms in the New Testament that *"God is not a God of disorder, but of peace"* (1 Corinthians 14:33). While this verse addresses chaos in worship, its principle extends beyond liturgy. God is not associated with confusion, unpredictability, or senselessness. Rather, His nature is expressed in harmony, balance, and coherence. What we often call the "laws of nature" or "mathematical constants" are, from a theological perspective, the laws and patterns God has established.

Step outside on a clear night and gaze upward. The stars move in predictable patterns. The moon waxes and wanes on a reliable schedule. The earth spins at a precise rate and orbits the sun in a mathematically consistent ellipse. None of this is arbitrary. The precision we observe in the universe is what allows science, and specifically mathematics, to describe it.

One of the clearest ways to observe divine order is through **mathematical patterns in nature**, and among the most beautiful of these is the **Fibonacci sequence**. This sequence: 0, 1, 1, 2, 3, 5, 8, 13, 21, 34…emerges when each number is the sum of the two preceding it. Simple in its construction, it appears everywhere: in the spirals of sunflower seeds, pinecones, hurricanes, galaxies, and the architecture of nautilus shells.

But why should such a simple numerical pattern appear so frequently in natural forms? Could this be coincidence, or does it point to something deeper? To the Christian mind, the answer lies in the nature of God Himself: orderly, consistent, and creative.

Closely related is the **Golden Ratio**, denoted by the Greek letter phi (φ), approximately equal to 1.618. Found by dividing consecutive Fibonacci numbers, this ratio is considered aesthetically pleasing and appears in art, architecture, and nature. The Parthenon in Greece, Leonardo da Vinci's

"Vitruvian Man," and even the proportions of the human body reflect this ratio. In nature, it's seen in flower petals, branching trees, and the spiral galaxies. This ratio is not just beautiful but mathematically inevitable and universally recurring.

Symmetry also plays a foundational role in the natural world. Snowflakes exhibit six-fold symmetry, spider webs form radial patterns, and even the bilateral symmetry of the human body speaks to a structured plan. Mathematical symmetry, reflected in geometric, algebraic, and even fractal forms, is not just pleasing to the eye. It provides stability, functionality, and resilience in biological organisms. The consistency with which symmetry occurs again points to intentionality behind design.

It is tempting to see these patterns as mere scientific facts. But to the believer, they are theological clues, evidences of a mind behind the math. As Kepler once said, *"The chief aim of all investigations of the external world should be to discover the rational order and harmony which has been imposed on it by God."*

Some critics might argue that nature also exhibits chaos, randomness, and destruction: earthquakes, disease, genetic mutations. But even chaos theory reveals hidden patterns. The **Mandelbrot set**, a complex mathematical figure, displays infinite complexity derived from a simple formula. The very fact that something as visually unpredictable as a fractal can be governed by precise equations suggests that chaos is not without its limits. It is contained, bounded, perhaps even allowed, for reasons we don't yet fully understand.

From a Christian perspective, the presence of disorder in the world is not a failure of God's design but a consequence of human sin and the fall (Romans 8:20-22). Yet even in a fallen world, the deeper patterns hold. Gravity still works. Pi remains irrational but constant. Fibonacci flowers still bloom. The sustaining order behind all things is never fully lost.

This divine order is reaffirmed in the prologue of John's Gospel: *"In the beginning was the Word, and the Word was with God, and the Word was God... Through him all things were made"* (John 1:1–3). The Greek word used for "Word" is *Logos*, which also means logic, reason, or principle. John identifies Jesus as the Logos, the rational structure underlying all existence. In this light, mathematics becomes not merely a human invention but a reflection of the divine Logos. To engage in mathematics is, in a sense, to engage with the mind of Christ.

Recognizing God as the Author of order and structure has profound implications for Christian education and personal faith. It means that disciplines like math and science are not secular by nature but sacred in origin. They are tools for exploring God's creation, not rivals to God's revelation.

For students, especially those who struggle to find relevance in math beyond tests and grades, this perspective offers a transformational shift. Math is not just about numbers on a page, it's about discovering how God has built the world. When we solve an equation, identify a pattern, or prove a theorem, we are participating in a divine activity: the search for truth.

For those inclined to worship and wonder, mathematics can become a spiritual experience. As the Psalmist writes, *"The heavens declare the glory of God; the skies proclaim the work of his hands"* (Psalm 19:1). That proclamation is written in the language of math: angles, distances, speeds, and cycles. And to the one who listens closely, that language sings of a Creator who is not only powerful but precise.

The universe is full of constants, unchanging numbers that form the foundation for physical laws. The speed of light, the gravitational constant, Planck's constant, and even the mathematical constant pi (π), these values remain the same regardless of time or place. Were they to change, even slightly, life would be impossible.

From a theological perspective, these constants are a kind of covenant. They testify to God's faithfulness, His reliability. Just as He promises never to change, so too does the universe He sustains. *"Jesus Christ is the same yesterday and today and forever"* (Hebrews 13:8). In a world where so much is shifting, the constancy of the universe reflects the constancy of its Maker.

The existence of such constants also speaks to a fine-tuned creation. Many physicists agree that if these values were even slightly different, the universe would collapse, stars wouldn't form, and life would be impossible. This phenomenon, often referred to as the **anthropic principle**, raises questions that science alone cannot answer. Why are the constants what they are? Why does the universe seem "rigged" in favor of life?

Christianity offers an answer: because a personal, purposeful Creator designed it that way.

To say that God is the Author of order and structure is to affirm that the universe is not an accident, nor is it opaque. It is legible. It can be studied, understood, and even marveled at through disciplines like mathematics. Every spiral in a sunflower, every line of symmetry in a snowflake, every orbital path of a planet speaks not only of science but of sacredness.

This is not a naive romanticism of mathematics, nor a misuse of theology to decorate science. It is a recognition that the patterns we find in the world point to a Patternmaker, that the laws we discover suggest a Lawgiver. Mathematics does not replace God; it reflects Him. And in this reflection, we are invited not only to reason but to worship.

III. The Language of Creation

From the earliest days of human curiosity, people have peered into the fabric of reality and found something unexpected, order. Beneath the rustling chaos of life, there exists a quiet logic. From the spiral of a galaxy to the tiny structure of a snowflake, there is something that speaks not just of beauty or elegance, but of a deeper truth, a language. And that language, as many have come to believe, is mathematics.

This observation is not new. Johannes Kepler, the great astronomer and devout Christian, once wrote, "The chief aim of all investigations of the external world should be to discover the rational order and harmony which has been imposed on it by God." In this sense, mathematics becomes more than a tool, it becomes a means of divine communication, a cipher for decoding the fingerprints of the Creator Himself. As we explore the patterns in nature, the fine-tuning of the universe, and the constancy of mathematical truths, we come to see that mathematics may very well be the language God used to write the universe.

Nature is a silent but eloquent speaker. It whispers the secrets of the divine through its patterns, forms, and structures. When we examine these repeating motifs, snowflakes, honeycombs, and orbits, we begin to see a rhythm to creation that is neither random nor accidental. Mathematics is not merely present in these examples; it is embedded, woven into their essence.

Every snowflake is unique, yet they all share a six-fold symmetry governed by the molecular structure of water. This balance of unity and individuality is striking. On a microscopic level, snowflakes are governed by fractal geometry, recursive patterns that emerge at every scale. Benoît Mandelbrot, the father of fractal geometry, described such structures as "roughness" that defies traditional Euclidean shapes. Yet they are precisely formed, mathematically patterned.

In Psalm 147:16, we read, *"He gives snow like wool; He scatters the frost like ashes."* The poetic rendering of snow in scripture resonates with the reality that each flake is a crystalline testament to God's attention to detail. The fact that each snowflake's pattern is both governed by physical laws and also distinct suggests a dual truth: the universe is ordered, but not mechanical; purposeful, but not rigid.

Fractals like those in snowflakes point to deeper spiritual realities. They demonstrate that even chaos, when viewed correctly, contains order. In theological terms, the fractal nature of snowflakes might remind us of God's ability to bring form from formlessness, just as He did in Genesis 1.

Among the most celebrated patterns in nature is the beehive, a structure built entirely from hexagons. This is no aesthetic accident. The hexagon is the most efficient shape for maximizing area while minimizing perimeter. It allows bees to store the greatest amount of honey using the least amount of wax.

This phenomenon has fascinated scientists and philosophers for centuries. The Roman scholar Marcus Terentius Varro proposed the "honeycomb conjecture," which was later proved mathematically in 1999 by Thomas C. Hales. The conjecture asserts that a hexagonal grid is the best way to divide a surface into regions of equal area with the least total perimeter.

The hexagon speaks to divine wisdom in design. Bees, operating without calculus or engineering degrees, build with perfect efficiency. Who taught them? Proverbs 6:6 exhorts us to "Go to the ant, you sluggard; consider its ways and be wise."

Likewise, we might go to the bee and learn about divine economy, a balance of strength, function, and beauty.

This organic geometry points us toward a God who values both utility and elegance, reminding us that the natural world is not only a resource but also a revelation.

In the vastness of space, one might expect randomness to reign. Yet the orbits of planets follow precise paths described by Kepler's laws and Newtonian mechanics. Planets move in ellipses, not circles, as first described in Kepler's First Law. These elliptical orbits can be predicted using mathematical equations, a truth that has stood unchallenged for centuries.

The idea that the universe could be so finely ordered, down to the movement of planets millions of miles away, inspired a generation of thinkers. Sir Isaac Newton, whose laws of motion and gravitation explained planetary behavior, was profoundly influenced by his belief in a rational God. He saw the mathematical order of the cosmos as direct evidence of a divine legislator.

Psalm 19:1 says, *"The heavens declare the glory of God, and the sky above proclaims His handiwork."* The mathematical predictability of the cosmos is a modern chime of that ancient song. As scientists send spacecraft across billions of miles using nothing but equations, we are reminded that the universe behaves as if it is governed, not by chance, but by intention.

In recent decades, scientists have observed something deeply puzzling: the physical constants of the universe appear to be precisely calibrated to support life. This observation has given rise to the **Anthropic Principle**, which posits that the universe's laws and parameters are not arbitrary, they are fine-tuned in such a way that observers like us can exist to contemplate them.

Consider the strength of the gravitational force. If gravity were slightly weaker, stars could not form; if it were slightly stronger, stars would burn too quickly and unevenly. Or take the electromagnetic force, if its strength varied by even a fraction, atoms could not form, let alone complex molecules or life.

Physicist Paul Davies once noted, "There is for me powerful evidence that there is something going on behind it all...It seems as though somebody has fine-tuned nature's numbers to make the Universe." Similarly, physicist Fred Hoyle, an agnostic, remarked that "a common-sense interpretation of the facts suggests that a super-intellect has monkeyed with physics."

For the believer, these "coincidences" are more than curious, they are confirmation. They point to a God who not only created, but calibrated the cosmos. Isaiah 45:18 declares, *"For thus says the Lord, who created the heavens... He established it; He did not create it empty, He formed it to be inhabited."*

The universe is not merely a backdrop; it is a habitat, painstakingly prepared for life. This fine-tuning suggests not only intelligence but intention. And mathematics is the blueprint of this intention.

To escape the implications of fine-tuning, some scientists propose the **multiverse**, the idea that ours is just one of countless universes, each with different physical laws. In such a scenario, we just happen to be in the one that works.

But this idea, while mathematically entertaining, remains speculative. It is unobservable and unfalsifiable. In contrast, the theistic explanation is both parsimonious and congruent with the evidence: the universe is finely tuned because it was finely designed.

Whether one interprets the anthropic principle philosophically or theologically, it demands a response. The fact that the universe permits not only life but also *intelligent* life, capable of discovering and understanding the laws that govern it, is one of the most profound signs of divine generosity.

There are numbers that recur in nature, architecture, music, and science, numbers that seem to have a metaphysical weight. Among these are π (pi), e (Euler's number), and φ (the golden ratio). These constants are not inventions; they are *discoveries*. They exist whether or not we observe them, suggesting that they are woven into the very structure of reality.

Pi (π) is the ratio of a circle's circumference to its diameter. It is an irrational number, stretching infinitely without repeating. And yet, it appears everywhere: in geometry, trigonometry, waves, statistics, and even quantum mechanics.

The circle, represented by pi, has long been seen as a symbol of eternity and perfection. In Christian theology, the circle has been used to represent God, without beginning or end. The fact that pi cannot be fully expressed, even with an infinite number of digits, might be seen as a mathematical metaphor for the divine: comprehensible in part, but ultimately beyond full human grasp.

Pi reminds us that the infinite lies just beneath the surface of the finite. It suggests that what we perceive as solid or simple is undergirded by profound complexity and depth.

Euler's number (e $\approx$ 2.718) arises in the study of exponential growth, decay, and compound interest. It is also irrational and appears in natural processes like population dynamics, radioactive decay, and even in the probability theory.

In theological reflection, it could be seen as a symbol of the laws that govern change, growth, death, and renewal. It encapsulates the rhythms of life and time. Whereas pi speaks of constancy, e speaks of transformation.

As Ecclesiastes reminds us, "To everything there is a season, and a time for every purpose under heaven." The presence of e in natural change reinforces the idea that God is not only the architect of order but also the author of seasons, of growth and passage.

The golden ratio ($\varphi \approx 1.618$) is a proportion found in art, architecture, nature, and the human body. It appears in the spirals of shells, the arrangement of petals, the structure of the Parthenon, and even the proportions of the human face.

Leonardo da Vinci used the golden ratio extensively in his art, and the Renaissance saw φ as a symbol of divine beauty. The reason is simple: the golden ratio creates balance and harmony that humans find inherently pleasing.

In theological terms, φ could be seen as God's aesthetic fingerprint. As Genesis tells us, *"God saw all that He had made, and it was very good."* The presence of φ in both organic and human design suggests that beauty is not merely subjective; it is embedded in creation.

The Apostle John begins his Gospel with, *"In the beginning was the Word (Logos), and the Word was with God, and the Word was God."* The Greek term *Logos* connotes reason, logic, and order. In declaring that the Logos was made flesh in Christ, John ties divine rationality directly to human experience.

Mathematics, as the language of logic, can be seen as a reflection of the Logos. The fact that we can understand the world mathematically, across cultures, languages, and centuries, suggests that reason is not a human invention, but a divine gift.

C.S. Lewis once said, "Men became scientific because they expected law in nature, and they expected law in nature because they believed in a Lawgiver." When we study mathematics, we do not merely manipulate symbols, we listen to the tune of a divine voice.

The patterns of snowflakes, the precision of orbits, the fine-tuning of constants, and the universality of mathematical truths all point to one conclusion: creation is not silent. It is speaking. It is rational. And it is beautiful.

Mathematics, in this light, is not a cold or sterile discipline. It is the music of the spheres, the architecture of the cosmos, the syntax of the Creator. It invites us not only to understand but to worship.

Romans 1:20 affirms this mystery: *"For since the creation of the world God's invisible qualities, His eternal power and divine nature, have been clearly seen, being understood from what has been made."* And what has been made is deeply, profoundly mathematical.

To engage with mathematics is to read a language older than time, written not in ink but in the stars, in the atoms, and in our very minds. It is a language that says, "Let there be light," and then goes on to calculate its speed.

In the language of numbers, God has not only written the laws of the universe, He has invited us to know Him through them.

IV. Logic, Proof, and Faith

Human beings are endowed with the capacity for reason and the longing for transcendence. At first glance, logic and faith may seem like opposing forces, one rooted in verifiable systems, the other in invisible hope. But in their deepest essence, both seek the same end: truth. While logic demands rigor, proof, and consistency, faith calls for trust in the unseen, the eternal, and the ineffable. Yet, both are driven by a deep human need to understand our place in the cosmos, to explore the foundations of existence, and to connect with something greater than ourselves. When viewed through a wider philosophical lens, logic and faith are not opposites but parallel approaches, often touching, sometimes overlapping, and always rooted in the desire to comprehend what lies beneath the surface of the visible world.

Every structured system, whether spiritual or scientific, begins with foundational assumptions. In mathematics, we call these **axioms**. An axiom is a self-evident truth or an assumed premise from which the rest of a logical framework is built. These are not proven within the system, they are accepted as starting points. Euclid, for instance, in his seminal work *Elements*, outlined five postulates that formed the foundation of classical geometry. One such postulate states that a straight line can be drawn from any point to any other point. This was not something to be proven, it was assumed, and from it the entire edifice of Euclidean geometry was constructed.

Religious and spiritual systems begin similarly, with certain truths that are not necessarily proven, but believed. In Christianity, for example, there is the foundational belief that God exists, that He is good, and that He created the universe with purpose. These are axioms of faith. They cannot be proven empirically, but they shape the way believers interpret the world, make moral decisions, and find meaning.

The similarity between these two kinds of axioms is striking. Both are foundational, both are unprovable within their systems, and both serve as lenses through which reality is understood. In both cases, these assumptions require a form of acceptance, a kind of intellectual surrender, not unlike a leap of faith.

To trust a mathematical system is to accept its axioms. To engage in a life of faith is to accept spiritual axioms. The journey that follows is then a process of working out the implications of these foundational beliefs.

Consider the reality that many mathematical truths are believed not because they are directly experienced or visible, but because they emerge logically from axioms and reasoning. For instance, most of us accept that there are infinitely many prime numbers. We cannot count them all, nor can we see infinity, but we accept it based on a rigorous logical proof first articulated by Euclid over two millennia ago. Similarly, we believe in the existence of irrational numbers such as π and $\sqrt{2}$ even though they cannot be fully written out or visually comprehended.

Belief in these truths, though rooted in logic, still involves a form of intellectual trust. We may not re-prove the theorems ourselves, but we trust in the soundness of the reasoning, the credibility of the mathematicians, and the consistency of the system.

This parallels how many religious believers come to trust spiritual truths. They may not have had personal theophanies or mystical experiences, but they trust in the integrity of sacred texts, the testimony of saints or prophets, and the inner coherence of a spiritual worldview. The distinction here is not one of rationality versus irrationality, but one of the kind of evidence and the framework in which it is accepted.

Moreover, just as mathematical truths can evoke wonder, such as the beauty of fractals, the elegance of Euler's identity, or the symmetry in number theory, so too can spiritual truths inspire awe, reverence, and transformation. Both engage the whole person, intellect and emotion, reason and imagination.

The Christian Scriptures offer a definition of faith in Hebrews 11:1: *"Now faith is the substance of things hoped for, the evidence of things not seen."* This idea, that something unseen can be so substantial as to ground our trust, resonates deeply with how mathematics operates.

No one has ever seen the number 7. We have seen seven objects, counted to seven, or represented 7 in symbols, but the number itself is an abstract idea. Yet we build entire systems of thought upon such unseen realities. The same is true for geometric concepts like lines without thickness, points without dimension, or planes without depth. These are not observable in the physical world, they are ideal forms. And yet, they guide architecture, physics, and engineering.

Similarly, in religious experience, believers trust in unseen realities: the soul, heaven, divine presence, and eternal purpose. These are not verifiable in the material sense, but they are treated as foundational to the meaning of life.

The parallel becomes even clearer when we examine how both systems deal with the limitations of proof. In mathematics, certain things are assumed to be true in order for the rest of the system to function. One does not "prove" an axiom, it is accepted. In faith, doctrines such as grace, salvation, or reincarnation (depending on the religion) are likewise accepted on the basis of authority, tradition, or inner conviction, rather than empirical demonstration.

Thus, faith is not contrary to reason, it is its counterpart. Both logic and faith move us forward, past the boundaries of what can be seen, and into the realm of what can be trusted. And in both systems, trust is not weakness, it is the soil from which understanding grows.

Perhaps one of the most profound intersections of mathematics and metaphysics comes in the 20th century, through the work of **Kurt Gödel**, whose **incompleteness theorems** shook the foundations of formal logic and mathematics. Gödel showed that in any sufficiently complex mathematical system, there will be statements that are **true** but **unprovable** within that system. In other words, no logical system can be both complete and consistent, it cannot prove all truths using only its own rules.

This was a humbling revelation. For centuries, mathematicians sought to construct a perfect system, a complete and airtight logic that could explain everything from first principles. Gödel showed that such a goal is fundamentally impossible. There will always be truths that transcend the system.

This insight resonates deeply with spiritual thought. The religious mind has always acknowledged the limits of reason. Theologians and mystics from all traditions, from Augustine and Aquinas to Rumi and Laozi, have spoken of a truth that surpasses understanding. The mystery of God, the experience of the infinite, or the reality of enlightenment cannot be captured by words or reason alone.

Gödel's work affirms that reason itself points beyond itself. There are truths that are real, but not reachable through logic alone. This is not to devalue reason, but to remind us of its limits. It is, in fact, a call to **intellectual humility**, one of the highest virtues in both science and spirituality.

Philosopher and mathematician Alfred North Whitehead once said, "The reason we can find unity in the universe is because the universe is built on the principle of the harmony of diversity." This suggests that no single approach, neither logic alone, nor faith alone, is sufficient to grasp the totality of truth.

Instead, they must dance together, like left and right hand, forming a union in the pursuit of wisdom.

Both logic and faith begin with a question: *Why?* Why is there something rather than nothing? Why does the universe operate according to laws? Why do humans long for meaning, beauty, and transcendence?

In mathematics, these questions often lead to the discovery of deeper patterns and relationships. We seek to quantify, model, and analyze. In faith, the same questions lead to contemplation, worship, and surrender. We seek to love, understand, and serve.

Both disciplines are animated by **wonder**. Wonder is the seed of all knowing. It is what moves the mathematician to spend decades solving a single problem. It is what draws the mystic into silence and solitude. Wonder is what opens the door to the sacred in every realm.

Moreover, both logic and faith are deeply communal. Mathematicians build upon the discoveries of others, and proofs are validated through peer consensus. Believers find strength in community, in shared rituals, and in traditions that span centuries. The pursuit of truth is never solitary, it is always embedded in relationship.

And in both cases, mystery remains. The more we discover, the more questions emerge. As physicist Richard Feynman once said, "I think nature's imagination is so much greater than man's, she's never going to let us relax." In the same way, the Divine is never fully captured by doctrine or ritual, the more we know, the more we stand in awe.

Throughout history, great thinkers have sought to bridge the gap between reason and revelation. Saint Anselm spoke of "faith seeking understanding." Maimonides explored how philosophy could clarify Jewish theology. Islamic scholar Al-Ghazali wrote about the role of reason in navigating spiritual insight. In Hindu thought, the Upanishads explore how knowledge (jnana) and devotion (bhakti) are two paths toward the same truth.

Modern thinkers continue this work. Theoretical physicists speak of the "elegance" of the cosmos. Mathematicians speak of "beauty" in equations. These are aesthetic judgments, evoking the same language that poets and prophets have used for centuries. There is something profoundly emotional about discovering a truth, whether through logic or through faith.

This suggests that our minds are not split between cold reason and irrational belief, but are deeply integrated. We are beings of thought and feeling, science and spirit, proof and poetry.

Perhaps this is why some of the greatest scientific minds, Kepler, Newton, Pascal, Einstein, were also people of profound metaphysical or spiritual interest. They saw no contradiction in seeking both the laws of nature and the source of those laws.

In truth, faith and logic are not enemies but siblings, born from the same human longing for meaning, shaped by the same desire to understand.

Whether approached by way of mathematical logic or metaphysical belief, truth is always more than we can grasp. Each system offers a glimpse, a facet, a language through which the Real is refracted. As the Apostle Paul once wrote, "Now we see through a glass, darkly, but then face to face" (1 Corinthians 13:12). This acknowledgement of partiality is not despair, it is an invitation to humility.

Similarly, the great Indian sage Ramanuja spoke of *tat tvam asi*, "that thou art" the unity of the soul with the divine, not as a rational proposition, but a spiritual reality that must be lived and realized. Like Gödel's theorem, it cannot be proven from within the system, it must be encountered.

We must be careful, then, not to idolize either logic or faith, as though one alone could deliver us to perfect understanding. Instead, we are called to a synthesis, a reverence for both mind and heart, proof and mystery, calculation and contemplation.

Just as the beauty of a sunset cannot be reduced to wavelengths, and yet those wavelengths are real, so too, the truth of the universe cannot be contained in formulas or dogmas, and yet those tools help us glimpse the Infinite.

In the end, logic and faith are two windows looking out onto the same light. Through logic, we trace the patterns that govern matter, space, and time. Through faith, we open ourselves to the mystery that breathes through it all. The more we learn from one, the more we appreciate the other.

V. Christian Mathematicians in History

Throughout the history of mathematics, many of its brightest minds were not only devoted to numbers, formulas, and geometric abstractions but also to a deep and abiding faith in God. For these individuals, mathematics was not just an intellectual discipline; it was a divine language, an ordered system that mirrored the rational structure of the universe crafted by a Creator. Let's explore the lives of three towering figures in the development of mathematics: **Blaise Pascal**, **Isaac Newton**, and **Johannes Kepler**, detailing how their Christian convictions shaped their work and worldview. Their contributions stand as a testimony to the possibility, even necessity, of integrating faith with intellectual rigor.

Blaise Pascal: Mathematician, Physicist, and Theologian

Blaise Pascal (1623–1662) was a French mathematician, physicist, inventor, philosopher, and theologian. A child prodigy, he was educated by his father, a tax collector with an intense interest in science. By the age of 16, Pascal had written a groundbreaking treatise on projective geometry, titled *Essai pour les coniques* (Essay on Conics). He later contributed to the development of probability theory, laying the groundwork for modern statistics and risk analysis alongside Pierre de Fermat.

Pascal also designed the Pascaline, an early mechanical calculator, and conducted pioneering work in fluid mechanics and pressure, formulating what we now call *Pascal's Law*. His investigations in the physical sciences often pushed the boundaries of contemporary understanding, and he was elected to the prestigious Académie française for his contributions.

Despite his early fame and success, Pascal experienced a profound spiritual crisis in 1654. On the night of November 23, he had a mystical experience that he documented in a note, later discovered sewn into his coat lining, known as the *Memorial*. It begins: "**FIRE. God of Abraham, God of Isaac, God of Jacob, not of the philosophers and savants.**" This moment marked a radical transformation in his life, shifting his focus from secular endeavors to theology and philosophy.

He joined the Jansenist movement, a Catholic reform branch emphasizing original sin, human depravity, and divine grace, concepts that resonated with Pascal's deepening sense of human frailty and the necessity of faith. His religious writings, most notably *Pensées* (Thoughts), reveal his philosophical brilliance and spiritual depth.

Pascal did not abandon mathematics after his conversion. Rather, he reframed it through a spiritual lens. His famous *Wager* argument is both a philosophical and probabilistic appeal to faith: If God exists, the believer gains everything; if not, he loses little. Thus, it is rational, even mathematically sound, to bet on God's existence. Here, Pascal employed his knowledge of probability theory not merely as an academic exercise but as a bridge between rationality and faith.

He saw the human condition as split between greatness and wretchedness, created in God's image yet fallen from grace. Mathematics, in his eyes, was a tool to comprehend the order and rationality of creation, even as the human heart remained restless without God. He famously said, "The heart has its reasons which reason knows nothing of."

Pascal's life reminds us that intellectual brilliance and deep faith are not mutually exclusive. They can exist in fruitful dialogue, each enriching the other. His legacy is not only the mathematical theorems that bear his name but also the philosophical insight that true understanding requires both logic and love.

Isaac Newton: Faith as the Foundation of Natural Law

Sir Isaac Newton (1642–1727) is often hailed as the greatest scientific mind of all time. His *Philosophiæ Naturalis Principia Mathematica*, published in 1687, revolutionized physics by outlining the laws of motion and universal gravitation. Newton also made significant advances in optics, inventing the reflecting telescope, and in mathematics, where he independently developed calculus (simultaneously with Leibniz).

These achievements laid the foundation for classical mechanics and provided a framework that governed the physical universe for over two centuries. Yet behind the towering intellect stood a man driven by intense spiritual convictions.

Newton was a devout Christian who spent more time studying the Bible than he did on science. His private writings, many of which remained unpublished in his lifetime, reveal a man who viewed the universe as a divine machine created by an all-wise, all-powerful God. For Newton, understanding nature was a way of understanding the Creator's mind.

He wrote extensively on theology and biblical prophecy, including a detailed study of the Book of Revelation and a fervent belief in a rational, orderly God who revealed Himself through both Scripture and nature. Newton once stated, *"This most beautiful system of the sun, planets, and comets could only proceed from the counsel and dominion of an intelligent and powerful Being."*

Newton believed that God's laws were immutable, and thus, nature operated like a clockwork universe governed by divine order. This belief in consistency and rationality underpinned his scientific work. Without a Creator who ordered all things, Newton argued, science would be impossible. He did not see his religious studies as separate from his scientific work, but rather as a unified pursuit of truth.

Newton's mathematical breakthroughs were driven by a desire to uncover the underlying order of creation. His laws of motion and gravitation demonstrated that the cosmos operated according to principles that could be described with precision, laws that did not replace God but revealed Him. He famously declared, *"Gravity explains the motions of the planets, but it cannot explain who sets the planets in motion."*

For Newton, mathematics was the divine language through which God wrote the universe. His studies were not merely academic or empirical but spiritual acts of devotion. Each calculation was, in a sense, a hymn of praise to the Creator of all things.

Even as he faced skepticism from Enlightenment thinkers who began to separate science from religion, Newton maintained that belief in God was essential to a full understanding of reality. The very existence of rational laws, he argued, pointed to a rational Lawgiver.

Johannes Kepler: Thinking God's Thoughts After Him

Johannes Kepler (1571–1630), a German astronomer and mathematician, is best known for his laws of planetary motion, which described the elliptical orbits of planets around the sun. His work built upon the observations of Tycho Brahe and paved the way for Newton's theory of universal gravitation.

Kepler's deep commitment to the heliocentric model advanced by Copernicus defied the prevailing geocentric views of the time. His revolutionary ideas placed him at odds with both scientific orthodoxy and ecclesiastical authorities, yet he pursued truth relentlessly, fueled by a spiritual conviction that studying the heavens was a sacred endeavor.

Kepler was a devout Lutheran who believed that God's glory was manifest in the harmony of the cosmos. He once wrote, "*I am merely thinking God's thoughts after Him.*" This phrase encapsulates his theological understanding of science, not as a purely human enterprise, but as participation in the divine intelligence.

His personal life was marked by difficulty, he faced poverty, political exile, and family tragedy. Nevertheless, his unwavering faith carried him through these trials. He believed that suffering had redemptive value and that all creation was ultimately under God's providence.

His religious convictions were not merely personal but informed his entire methodology. In his *Harmony of the World* (1619), Kepler combined his love of mathematics with a mystical belief in cosmic order, suggesting that the movements of the planets formed a kind of celestial music, a harmonious reflection of divine beauty.

Kepler believed that mathematics was the key to unlocking God's design in creation. He viewed the geometric patterns and ratios in the cosmos as fingerprints of divine authorship. For him, understanding these patterns was a spiritual act, akin to prayer or worship.

In his scientific writings, Kepler often employed theological language. He saw the universe not as a chaotic or arbitrary machine but as a reflection of divine harmony and purpose. Even when his findings challenged church teachings or traditional dogma, he remained steadfast in his belief that truth, scientific and theological, ultimately converged in God.

His work inspired generations of scientists and theologians alike. By demonstrating that faith and reason could coexist, Kepler offered a powerful model for intellectual inquiry rooted in reverence and humility.

Common Themes Across Lives

Despite their differences in temperament, geography, and religious affiliation, Pascal, Newton, and Kepler shared several common beliefs:

God as the Source of Order

All three believed that the universe operated according to divinely ordained principles and that mathematics was the language of this order.

Science as a Spiritual Vocation

None of them saw science as separate from faith. Their work was driven by a desire to glorify God, understand His creation, and make His wisdom known.

Humility in Discovery

Though brilliant, each man approached his work with humility, recognizing the limitations of human understanding and the infinite majesty of the Creator.

The Moral Dimension of Knowledge

For these thinkers, knowledge was not neutral; it carried ethical and spiritual implications. True understanding required both intellectual honesty and spiritual discernment.

In sum, their faith did not hinder their mathematical progress, it enriched it. Pascal's theology deepened his reflections on probability and human uncertainty. Newton's belief in divine law inspired his search for universal principles. Kepler's mystical view of harmony guided his discovery of planetary motion. Their convictions provided a coherent framework within which their scientific inquiries took place.

This synthesis challenges the false dichotomy often drawn between science and religion. For these men, to study nature was to study God. Mathematics was not a barrier to faith, but a bridge.

In an age that often pits faith and science against each other, the lives of Blaise Pascal, Isaac Newton, and Johannes Kepler offer a compelling counter-narrative. They demonstrate that faith can inspire rigorous inquiry, and that science can deepen spiritual wonder. These Christian mathematicians did not compartmentalize their lives; they integrated their love for God with their passion for discovery.

Their legacies invite us to consider that the pursuit of truth is holistic. It involves not only the mind but also the soul. They remind us that at the heart of both mathematics and faith is a deep longing, for order, for meaning, for transcendence.

Mathematics, in its precision and abstraction, has often been seen as the language of the universe. Its axioms, theorems, and symmetries define and describe everything from the smallest particles to the movement of galaxies. Yet, when we peer into the depths of mathematical truths, we do not merely uncover elegant structures, we glimpse something beyond. In the ordered patterns, unchanging laws, and timeless beauty of mathematics, many have seen the fingerprints of the Divine. The finite symbols and equations point, in their own way, toward the infinite, toward God Himself.

Throughout this exploration, we have seen how Christian mathematicians were not merely scientists or theorists but spiritual seekers. For them, mathematics was not isolated from theology. Instead, it was interwoven with their understanding of creation, truth, and God's character. The harmony, logic, and consistency found in math resonated deeply with their faith in a rational Creator. This conviction did not hinder their discoveries; it fueled them. The pursuit of mathematical knowledge became a sacred act, an offering of the mind to the Author of reason.

To study mathematics is, in a way, to participate in divine contemplation. When we engage with numbers, patterns, and relationships, we are not just playing with abstract concepts. We are exploring the very structure of creation. This pursuit, when anchored in faith, becomes a kind of worship. It is an act of reverence to trace the laws that God has written into the fabric of reality. In mathematics, we do not invent truth; we discover it. And in doing so, we are drawn to the One who is the source of all truth.

St. Augustine once wrote, *"The numbers by which we reckon are not the same as the things which we number, yet the numbers are eternal and unchanging."* He saw in mathematics a reflection of the eternal mind of God, a glimpse into the order and permanence that lies beyond our temporal world. Numbers do not decay. Truth in mathematics does not shift with culture or emotion. In this way, math mirrors the constancy and faithfulness of God Himself.

C.S. Lewis, too, reflected on the profound connection between the rational and the divine. In *Mere Christianity*, he wrote, *"If the whole universe has no meaning, we should never have found out that it has no meaning."* The very ability to reason, to discover consistent laws and to apply mathematical thinking, speaks of a world imbued with meaning, meaning that must come from a higher source.

And perhaps most poetically, the German mathematician and astronomer Johannes Kepler, in speaking of his astronomical discoveries, wrote: *"I am merely thinking God's thoughts after Him."* This humble statement captures the spirit of all those who see mathematics not just as a tool, but as a sacred endeavor. For Kepler, Newton, Pascal, and many others, their work in mathematics was not an end in itself, it was a window into the mind of God.

In today's world, mathematics continues to drive innovation, unlock secrets of nature, and solve complex problems. But for those with eyes of faith, it remains more than a discipline. It is a testimony. The infinite series, the irrational numbers, the perfect geometries, all are signs pointing us beyond themselves. They whisper of the eternal.

When we encounter infinity in math, whether in a converging sequence or in the boundlessness of π, we are invited to consider the Infinite Being. The one who set the laws in motion, who upholds all things by the word of His power, and who imbues even abstract constructs with meaning. Math becomes a bridge between the created and the Creator.

As we reflect on the unity of the finite and the infinite, the temporal and the eternal, let us remember that all truth is God's truth. Whether discovered through Scripture or through science, whether glimpsed in the stained glass of a cathedral or in the elegance of an equation, truth leads us to the same place: to awe, to humility, to worship.

In the words of poet George Herbert:

A man that looks on glass,

On it may stay his eye;

Or if he pleaseth, through it pass,

And then the heav'n espy.

Mathematics is such a glass. We may stop at its surface, marveling at its clarity and precision. Or we may look through it and see the grandeur of the God who designed it all.

In the end, the infinite points to the eternal. And through the study of the finite, we draw near to the Infinite One.

Reflective Questions:

Where have you seen patterns in nature or numbers that made you pause and sense something greater, something divine, behind the design?

_____

_____

_____

_____

In what ways can the precision and order of mathematics deepen your understanding of God's character and the way He interacts with creation?

_____

_____

_____

_____

How might viewing mathematical laws as part of God's language shift the way you approach learning, logic, or even your doubts?

_____

_____

_____

_____

Chapter 2
Chemistry and the Elements of Life

I. The Divine Architecture of Matter

Before the dawn of language, before ink met parchment, there was a language unspoken yet ever present, etched into the very bones of creation. It is the language of chemistry. Molecules whispered into form, atoms holding hands in quiet obedience, reactions set in motion by invisible commands; this is the language through which the Creator sculpted reality. And though we cannot see Him with our eyes, His fingerprints rest upon every electron, every carbon chain, every rhythmic dance of energy and form.

Everything we know, everything we see, and even what we cannot: our breath, our bones, the stars that pulse in the dark silence of the cosmos, is made of matter. Matter is the substance of God's artwork. It is the clay in the Potter's hand. From the tiniest particle, unseen and elusive, to the grandeur of galaxies stitched across the night sky, matter speaks. It speaks of purpose, of balance, of intentional design.

An atom may seem inconsequential, too small to warrant awe. Yet within its nucleus burns a force so profound it holds the universe together. Protons, neutrons, electrons, all in their precise places, dancing to a rhythm set long before man took his first breath. How could such order be accidental? How could such elegance be without Composer?

Chemistry teaches us that atoms bond because they lack wholeness. They seek stability, much like the soul seeks its Maker. Hydrogen leans into oxygen, and water is born, essential for life. Simple. Miraculous. Divine.

When substances meet and change, when bonds break and reform, we call it a chemical reaction. But in those moments of transformation lies a metaphor for grace itself. For what is salvation but a holy reaction? The old is broken; the new is born. A sinner meets the Savior, and the very nature of the soul is altered.

Combustion, fermentation, rust, all reactions governed by laws, yet open to interpretation by the eyes of wonder. The burning of wood releases warmth; the rising of bread gives nourishment. In every change, in every flicker of reaction, God's handiwork is present. He is the unseen catalyst behind every moment of becoming.

If God spoke the universe into existence, then chemistry is the script of that holy utterance. Each element, each compound, is a syllable in the vast poetry of life. The periodic table, so often confined to dusty textbooks and forgotten high school lectures, is a hymn of order and brilliance. Hydrogen, helium, carbon, nitrogen, they are not merely names, but notes in a song billions of years in the making.

The elegance of this language is not random. It was not flung into being. It was whispered. Crafted. Spoken with care. "Let there be..." was not only a command but a composition.

The laws of chemistry, so precise, so unyielding, are a reflection of God's nature. He is not a God of chaos, but of order. The same God who separated light from darkness also separated one element from another, assigning each its unique properties, affinities, and behaviors.

Let us not forget the pioneers who saw no conflict between the microscope and the Bible, between the laboratory and the sanctuary. Robert Boyle, the father of modern chemistry, once wrote that the study of nature was an act of worship. He believed that understanding the properties of gases was no less holy than reading Scripture, for both revealed the mind of God.

Other Christian chemists followed in his footsteps. Sir Humphry Davy, who discovered new elements, yet never ceased to marvel at the majesty behind them; George Washington Carver, who found hundreds of uses for the peanut, saying, "I love to think of nature as an unlimited broadcasting station, through which God speaks to us every hour, if we only will tune in."

These men did not separate their science from their faith. They built bridges with every discovery, connecting mind to spirit, reason to reverence.

II. The Periodic Table of Providence

In the silent order of things, there exists a table, not carved in marble or etched on ancient scrolls, but born of centuries of inquiry, illuminated by the fire of stars and the questions of men. The Periodic Table. To some, it is a mere grid, a checklist of atomic ingredients. But to those who observe with both mind and soul, it is more than a table. It is a window into the language of God, a revelation of order behind the veil of matter, a theological manuscript written in the grammar of physics.

At first glance, the periodic table may appear austere, a regimented lattice of boxes and numbers. But behind its surface lies a depth of symmetry and foresight that rivals the most intricate music, the most profound theology.

Dmitri Mendeleev, the devout Russian chemist, did not randomly arrange the elements; he recognized an underlying logic, what he called a "chemical periodicity." He left gaps in his table, predicting the existence of elements yet to be discovered, and their properties, many of which were later confirmed with astounding accuracy. Science did not create this order; it uncovered it.

This regularity reflects **quantum principles** at work. Each element finds its place according to the atomic number of protons in its nucleus, but the true elegance is in how this correlates with electron configuration, chemical behavior, and reactivity. Elements in the same column share **valence electrons**, the outermost electrons that govern chemical bonding.

For example:

- **Group 1 elements** (alkali metals) all have one valence electron and react vigorously with water.

- **Group 17 elements** (halogens) crave one more electron to complete their outer shell and thus bond readily with metals.

- **Group 18** (noble gases) have full electron shells and thus remain inert, self-contained, whole.

This order arises from the **quantum mechanical structure of atoms**, the arrangement of electrons into orbitals and subshells (s, p, d, f), following the **Pauli exclusion principle, Hund's rule**, and **Aufbau principle**. These are not chaotic behaviors; they are lawful, rational, even poetic.

How can such abstract order, which governs all matter, arise by accident? Is this not a theme of Logos: divine reason, divine logic, sewn into the bones of the universe?

Zooming into each atom reveals a microcosm of order. The nucleus, densely packed with protons and neutrons, is surrounded by electron clouds held in place by **electromagnetic force,** a fundamental force of nature. These particles are not stationary, but follow **quantum probability distributions** governed by the **Schrödinger equation**.

And yet, despite the probabilistic nature of quantum mechanics, macroscopic predictability emerges. The periodic table reflects this emergent order in several profound ways:

- **Atomic radius** decreases across a period due to increasing nuclear charge, which pulls electrons closer.

- **Ionization energy**, the energy required to remove an electron, increases across a period and decreases down a group, following a precise mathematical trend.

- **Electronegativity**, which describes an atom's tendency to attract electrons, follows a predictable pattern, fluorine being the most electronegative, cesium the least.

This fine-tuning allows molecules to form with consistent angles, bond lengths, and energies. Life requires molecules that are not just stable, but specific, **DNA, hemoglobin, chlorophyll**, each with structures dependent on atomic behavior.

If the **strong nuclear force** were slightly weaker, atoms would disintegrate. If **electromagnetic force** were slightly stronger, chemical bonding would be too rigid for life. Physicist Paul Davies calls this "**bio-friendliness**" of the universe one of the great wonders of modern science.

As theologian and scientist John Polkinghorne once said, "The intelligibility of the universe is not only a mystery but a gift."

In the Book of Genesis, God speaks the world into being. But what responds? Not vague abstraction, but elemental matter, **hydrogen**, the simplest and most abundant element in the cosmos. Formed seconds after the Big Bang, hydrogen became the building block of stars, which, through **stellar nucleosynthesis**, created helium, carbon, oxygen, nitrogen, the atoms necessary for life.

This process is no accident. The carbon atom, critical to life, forms only because of a precise nuclear resonance level in the carbon nucleus known as the **Hoyle state**, predicted by astrophysicist Fred Hoyle, who was so startled by its necessity for life that he remarked, "A commonsense interpretation of the facts suggests that a superintellect has monkeyed with physics."

Is it mere chance that carbon can form four bonds, making it uniquely suited for complexity, diversity, and resilience? Is it coincidence that **iron**, forged in supernovae, is not only magnetic and strong, but essential in hemoglobin, ferrying oxygen through our blood?

- **Phosphorus** (P) forms the backbone of **DNA and RNA**.

- **Sulfur** is essential in **protein folding** via disulfide bridges.

- **Calcium** builds bones, but also sends **neurotransmitter signals** in our brains.

- Even trace elements like **zinc** and **copper** play roles in **enzymatic reactions**, without which life would stop.

Each element has its place. Each fulfills a role. From **helium** cooling MRI machines, to **silicon** powering the microchips of our age, to **gold** conducting electrons in our devices, the elements are not static. They are alive with purpose.

It is not anti-science to see design; it is the result of awe. Albert Einstein once said, "The most incomprehensible thing about the universe is that it is comprehensible." The periodic table does not diminish faith, it deepens it. It reveals a Creator who is not only majestic but meticulous. Who creates not just stars but quarks. Not just galaxies but glucose.

In the periodic table, we find a covenant of consistency, laws that govern the cosmos with grace and regularity.

III. Water, Life, and the Breath of God

In the beginning, when the earth was formless and void, Scripture tells us that the Spirit of God hovered over the waters. Before light, before land, before language, there was water. And even now, thousands of years later, water remains the rhythm of creation, the lifeblood of the earth, and the whisper of divine breath in every living thing.

At the heart of life's chemistry lies a molecule so simple, yet so profound: H_2O. Two hydrogen atoms bound to one oxygen atom, not in a straight line, but in an angle of 104.5°, a seemingly modest tilt that changes everything. This bent geometry gives rise to **polarity**: the oxygen end carries a slight negative charge, and the hydrogens a slight positive charge. Like a magnet, water attracts itself and the world around it.

Because of this polarity, water forms **hydrogen bonds**: fleeting, gentle connections between molecules. These bonds give water its remarkable properties:

- **Cohesion and surface tension**, allowing insects to walk on water and trees to draw water to their tallest branches.

- **High specific heat**, enabling oceans to buffer climate and the body to maintain homeostasis.

- **Excellent solvency**, making water the "universal solvent," capable of dissolving salts, sugars, gases, and more, carrying nutrients and messages across every cell membrane.

These properties are not incidental; they are essential. Without them, enzymes would not fold, cells could not survive, blood could not flow, and life, as we know it, would not exist.

Is it mere chance that water behaves this way? Or is it evidence of a Creator who designed even the invisible forces between molecules with loving intention?

Water does not merely sustain the body, it washes the soul. Throughout Scripture, water is more than element; it is symbol, it is promise.

- In **Genesis**, the Spirit moves upon the waters.

- In **Exodus**, the Red Sea parts to deliver God's people.

- In **the Gospels**, Jesus is baptized in the Jordan, anointed not with oil but with water and Spirit.

- In **Revelation**, a river of life flows from God's throne, clear as crystal, offering healing to the nations.

Baptism is not simply a ritual, it is a declaration that we are buried with Christ and rise anew, washed clean, reborn. The very same molecule that makes our blood flow also signifies the washing away of sin. Water is God's physical provision for life and His spiritual symbol of renewal.

God is not divided in His giving. The same hands that shaped the stars also carved the rivers. The same breath that inspired the prophets animates the atoms.

Water illustrates this harmony: It hydrates and it heals, it flows through veins and Scriptures alike. Jesus, weary by a well, told a Samaritan woman, "Whoever drinks of the water I give will never thirst." (John 4:14) He was speaking of the Spirit, but the metaphor is layered. Our bodies are over **70% water**, and so are our spirits dependent on the living water that is Christ.

In every drop of rain, in every glass we lift to our lips, we encounter a holy intersection, where chemistry and covenant meet, where the Creator whispers, "I sustain you."

In chemistry, there are **covalent bonds**, where atoms share electrons, an image of mutual giving. There are **ionic bonds**, where one atom gives and the other receives, an image of sacrificial love.

Is this not a mirror of the relationships we are called to as believers? Marriage, friendship, community, each one a delicate dance of give and take, of shared burdens and poured-out grace.

Covalent bonds are strongest when electrons are shared equally. So too, relationships thrive in balance. But sometimes, love gives more than it receives. Just as sodium surrenders an electron to chloride to form salt, preserving and flavoring the earth, so Christ gave all that we might live.

These invisible bonds hold not only molecules together but are metaphors for unity in the Body of Christ.

Water molecules stick together. That is their nature, **hydrogen bonding** draws them toward one another, over and over, forming streams, lakes, oceans. Creation reflects communion.

Likewise, we were not made to walk alone. "Just as the body is one and has many parts… so it is with Christ." (1 Corinthians 12:12) We are cells in a living Body. Dependent. Interconnected. Flowing together in purpose.

God's covenant with His people is a bond stronger than any molecule. Through Christ, we are joined, not only to Him but to each other. Bound in Spirit, like atoms in a great and holy molecule, fulfilling a greater design.

When we study chemistry, we find that nothing exists in isolation. Molecules react with other molecules. Energy is transferred, transformed. Systems balance. Life thrives in interdependence.

Likewise, the Church, though many parts, functions as one. Just as the hydrogen in our breath once burned in stars, we are reminded that we are part of something eternal, cosmic, divine.

In the chemical elegance of water, in its quiet, miraculous work, we see God's fingerprints, subtle, yet undeniable. And in every baptism, in every rainfall, in every tear, we remember: His breath still moves over the waters.

IV. Energy, Entropy, and Reactions

In the visible and invisible workings of the universe, energy is never truly lost, only transformed. This principle, rooted in the First Law of Thermodynamics, is more than a law of physics; it speaks to something deeper, something spiritual. Just as matter shifts form and energy changes state, the soul undergoes its own transformation, sanctification, healing, redemption. The parallel between the physical and the spiritual is neither metaphor nor poetry alone; it is written into the structure of reality itself.

Chemical reactions offer a tangible window into this mystery. In exothermic reactions, energy is released into the surroundings. The combustion of magnesium, for example, produces a brilliant white flame, a striking image of power being expelled from matter. This is akin to what happens when we let go of sin or experience a spiritual breakthrough, energy is released, sometimes dramatically, sometimes quietly, and the environment around us is affected. It brings to mind moments

46

of deep worship, repentance, or even revival, when something within is burned away and something brighter remains.

By contrast, endothermic reactions absorb energy from their surroundings. The reaction between barium hydroxide and ammonium chloride is a striking case. When these two compounds are mixed, the reaction becomes so cold it can freeze a beaker to a wooden block. There's no flash or fire, just silence and a mysterious chill. Yet, beneath the surface, transformation is happening. Likewise, there are seasons of the soul that feel frozen, quiet, even numb. These times can be easily mistaken for spiritual stagnation. But like the endothermic reaction, something is shifting inside us. The energy we absorb through trials, endurance, prayer, and quiet faith is not wasted. God often works most powerfully in the hidden, cold, silent places where we believe nothing is happening.

All transformation, whether chemical or spiritual, requires energy input. This is true for sanctification. In the same way that chemical reactions need activation energy to get started, spiritual transformation often requires the heat of trials. The book of James speaks to this mystery: "Count it all joy when you fall into various trials, knowing that the testing of your faith produces endurance." Faith acts as a catalyst, it is not consumed in the reaction, but facilitates the change. It holds the process together and gives it direction. The energy of pain, struggle, and waiting becomes fuel for growth.

Yet in the midst of change, another force is at work, entropy. The Second Law of Thermodynamics tells us that in an isolated system, disorder increases over time. Without intervention, things fall apart. Systems degrade. Stars die, cells break down, relationships weaken. This is the story of a fallen world. We see it in rust, in aging, in sorrow. And yet, there is an opposing force. Life persists. Order emerges. Beauty is born in unlikely places. Scientific thought experiments like Maxwell's Demon illustrate the idea that for order to arise, there must be an external force, a non-random actor that intervenes. In the same way, God is the divine intervener. In a world spiraling toward chaos, He is the one who holds all things together. Hebrews tells us that Christ sustains all things by His powerful word. He is not only the creator but also the constant sustainer, the invisible hand that maintains structure where disorder should reign.

The persistence of life itself defies entropy. Consider the human body. It maintains homeostasis, an internal equilibrium that resists the pull toward disorder, by expending energy constantly. Cells use adenosine triphosphate (ATP) to maintain their shape, replicate DNA, and transport vital materials. Without a continual supply of energy, order collapses. Spiritually, we are no different. Our souls require nourishment, consistency, and divine energy. Scripture, prayer, worship, and communion with God are not optional accessories to life, they are the energy inputs that prevent spiritual decay.

Even the plants that blanket the earth resist entropy daily. Through photosynthesis, they capture light energy from the sun and use it to convert carbon dioxide and water into sugars, stored energy that supports all higher forms of life. This endothermic process is a quiet miracle that keeps the world alive. It reminds us that God's sustenance is not always loud or visible. Sometimes it is as subtle as a leaf turning sunlight into sugar. Yet without it, life would vanish.

From a spiritual lens, God's power is evident in both the slow processes and the explosive moments. There are times when transformation looks like a magnesium strip bursting into flame: sudden, brilliant, undeniable. And there are other times when it resembles photosynthesis or chemical freezing: slow, quiet, and hidden from view. Both are valid. Both are sacred. Both are real.

The First Law of Thermodynamics states that energy cannot be created or destroyed, it can only be transformed. Likewise, in the economy of God, nothing is wasted. Romans tells us that in all things, God works for the good of those who love Him. Every wound, every loss, every setback becomes material for redemption. The past isn't erased, but reformed into something useful. One might compare this to the Haber process, which is a chemical reaction that synthesizes ammonia from nitrogen and hydrogen under intense heat and pressure. Naturally, this reaction would rarely occur. But in controlled, high-pressure environments, it becomes possible. The result? Ammonia, used in fertilizers that sustain life on Earth. The process is violent, demanding, and unnatural, yet it gives birth to the conditions that make nourishment possible. So too with redemption. Under the right conditions: pressure, heat, and divine intervention, what was once inert or even harmful becomes life-giving.

The laws of physics and chemistry are not in conflict with faith, they whisper its mysteries. They remind us that transformation requires sacrifice, that order is not spontaneous, and that endurance is not a passive state but an active resistance to entropy.

V. Light, Electrons, and Divine Illumination

Light is the most ancient witness to creation. Before anything else was spoken into existence, light was called forth: "Let there be light." Genesis tells us that God separated light from darkness, not merely illuminating the void, but establishing the fundamental duality between chaos and order, hiddenness and revelation. And remarkably, thousands of years later, when science began to explore the nature of the universe, it was light again that revealed the most profound truths. The particle that carries light, the photon, is massless, yet it defines visibility, energy, and life. Photons travel at 299,792,458 meters per second, the fastest speed known in the universe. Time slows down for anything approaching that speed, a strange but consistent conclusion of Einstein's special relativity. At the speed of light, time stops altogether. It is no coincidence that the Bible repeatedly refers to God as light, timeless, present in all places at once, never aging, and never bound by the entropy that consumes everything else.

Light is both particle and wave. This duality baffled physicists for decades. The famous double-slit experiment demonstrated that photons behave as waves when unobserved, creating interference patterns on a detection screen. But when scientists attempted to measure which slit the photon passed through, the pattern collapsed, and the photon behaved like a particle instead. This phenomenon is called wave-function collapse, and it suggests that observation influences reality. Though interpretations vary, the experiment hints at a universe responsive to awareness. Some Christian physicists have speculated, though carefully, that the idea resonates with faith: that the eye of the observer, the presence of mind, even the divine consciousness itself, might play a role in sustaining what is real.

At the atomic level, light interacts with electrons, the carriers of charge. When photons strike a metal surface with sufficient energy, they can dislodge electrons, a process known as the photoelectric effect. This phenomenon was famously explained by Albert Einstein in 1905 and earned him the Nobel Prize. The energy of each photon is quantized, determined by its frequency, not its brightness. This discovery shattered classical ideas and launched quantum theory. But it also quietly parallels a spiritual principle: illumination, true spiritual awakening, does not come from intensity or emotional fervor, but from clarity and precision of truth. Just as a single high-frequency photon can liberate an electron, a single word from God, a single verse of Scripture, can release someone from bondage.

John 1 iterates the Genesis narrative with scientific elegance: "In the beginning was the Word... In Him was life, and that life was the light of all mankind. The light shines in the darkness, and the darkness has not overcome it." From a cosmological standpoint, darkness is not a thing in itself, it is merely the absence of light. Cold, similarly, is the absence of heat. These are not forces but conditions. Spiritually, the same is true: evil is not a force equal to God, it is a distortion, a void, a deviation from what is true and good. Just as photons illuminate and bring order, God's Word cuts through confusion and brings life.

Throughout history, many scientists have embraced this divine light alongside their scientific endeavors. One such figure was Robert Boyle, often called the father of modern chemistry. He not only developed the gas laws that describe pressure and volume but also funded Bible translations and missionary work. Boyle's personal writings reveal that he saw no contradiction between his faith and his scientific work, in fact, he viewed science as a means of worship. His "Christian Virtuoso" treatise advocated for scientists to remain devout and morally upright, believing that discovering God's design in nature would lead to reverence.

Another example is James Clerk Maxwell, the Scottish physicist who unified electricity, magnetism, and light into a single theory of electromagnetism. Maxwell's equations, four elegant differential formulas, are the foundation of our understanding of light and radio waves. Yet Maxwell was also a devout Christian who wrote poems and essays about his faith. In a letter to a friend, he wrote, "I think men of science as well as other men need to learn from Christ, and I think Christians whose minds are scientific are bound to study science that their view of the glory of God may be as extensive as their being is capable."

Even in the 20th and 21st centuries, the tradition of praying scientists continues. Dr. Henry F. Schaefer III, a quantum chemist and five-time Nobel Prize nominee, has written extensively on the intersection of science and belief. In lectures and writings, Schaefer asserts that many of the greatest scientists, Newton, Kepler, Faraday, Pasteur, were driven by their love for God and saw their work as uncovering divine order. He cites his own experience in computational chemistry as a space for prayer and reflection, where the mathematical intricacies of molecular orbitals bring him awe and humility before the Creator.

In the lab, ethics is not merely a guideline, it is a compass that reflects the soul of the researcher. The rise of genetic engineering, AI, and quantum computing presents humanity with the tools of tremendous power. But as the Bible warns, knowledge without wisdom is dangerous. The ethical dilemmas surrounding technologies like CRISPR, embryonic research, and surveillance algorithms are not technical problems but moral ones. The scientific method is a tool; it cannot tell us whether we ought to do something, only whether it is possible. Here is where faith is not a hindrance but a necessary safeguard. A scientist grounded in truth, humility, and reverence for life is one who sees beyond data points. They ask not only "What can I do?" but "What should I do?"

Integrity in scientific research has often been tested under pressure. In 1989, two scientists, Stanley Pons and Martin Fleischmann, claimed to have achieved cold fusion at room temperature. The news was sensational. Yet when other scientists tried to replicate the results, the findings collapsed under scrutiny. The rush for fame had overtaken the rigor of truth. Contrast that with the quiet work of Rosalind Picard, an MIT professor and Christian who leads affective computing research. She has spoken publicly about how her faith shapes her ethical stance on the responsible use of AI, emphasizing dignity, transparency, and compassion.

The light of scientific discovery, like the light of faith, must be handled with humility. It reveals, but it also blinds, if stared at too long without reverence. In Isaiah's vision, the seraphim cover their faces before the radiance of God. In science, too, the more we uncover, the more we realize how little we know. Quantum mechanics, with its probabilistic nature and hidden variables, has not answered every question. Instead, it has humbled our assumptions. And so, the praying scientist does not see mystery as failure, but as invitation.

Faith does not reject science, it makes it human. It anchors data to meaning. It reminds us that photons may show us the structure of the cosmos, but only love illuminates the soul. Light travels unimpeded through a vacuum, but it bends when it passes through different media, a phenomenon called refraction. Likewise, truth may be absolute, but its reception is shaped by the lens of our hearts. Let our hearts, then, be pure lenses, so that light may pass through undistorted.

In the end, the study of photons, electrons, and fields is not merely an academic pursuit, it is a sacred act. The One who said "Let there be light" continues to shine. Every illuminated atom, every spark of fluorescence, every qubit entanglement whispers of a greater reality. The Light of the world has come, not only to show us what is, but to reveal who we are. And in that light, we see clearly.

In every chemical bond, in the nature of light, energy, and matter, we glimpse not only the mechanics of a created universe but the character of its Creator. Scientific inquiry, at its best, does not replace faith, it deepens it. The disciplines of chemistry and light reveal a cosmos that is both ordered and mysterious, governed by precision yet open to wonder. Just as reactions require energy to break bonds and form new ones, so too does transformation in our lives require divine intervention and surrender. As entropy marches on and systems tend toward disorder, we see in Christ the One who sustains all things, who brings light into darkness, and restores brokenness to purpose. To study the natural world is to trace the outline of the divine, and to walk by faith is to move forward with eyes open, guided not only by what is seen, but by the light that reveals all things.

Reflective Questions

How does knowing that your body is made from the same elements found in stars affect your sense of connection to creation, and to the Creator?

_____

_____

_____

_____

In what ways do the interactions between elements, so precise, so purposeful, reflect the intentional design and order of God's work in your own life?

_____

_____

_____

_____

Can you see God's presence not just in miracles, but in the quiet, invisible reactions sustaining your breath, your heartbeat, and your being?

_____

_____

_____

_____

Chapter 3
Particle Physics and the Invisible Eye of the Beholder

I. A Brief Primer on Particle Physics:

Beneath the stars above, the soil below, and the breath within us lies a hidden world that is utterly invisible, yet more real than anything we see. This is the empire of particle physics, where the universe is not built from solid objects but from shimmering forces and fleeting particles. Quarks, leptons, bosons, the elusive Higgs field, these are not just scientific curiosities. They are the alphabet of reality, the silent code behind all creation. This is the unseen engine of the cosmos, where the physical and the divine whisper to one another in the language of existence.

The particles studied in modern physics are unimaginably small, far smaller than atoms, and yet they shape every aspect of material reality. They determine the properties of matter, the forces of nature, and the unfolding behavior of the cosmos from the moment of the Big Bang to this very instant. These particles are not static pebbles drifting in a cosmic void; they are dynamic entities governed by mathematical laws, participating in a strange and beautiful dance of creation.

For many, science and faith exist in tension, if not outright conflict. But this chapter dares to suggest a different possibility, that particle physics, when viewed with both humility and imagination, can deepen rather than diminish the Christian understanding of the universe. Far from eroding faith, the insights of modern physics can be a source of wonder that draws us into deeper reverence for the divine. The very laws and patterns discovered in the subatomic world suggest an order, a harmony, and a purposeful design that resonate with the biblical portrait of a Creator who speaks the universe into being and sustains it moment by moment.

Hebrews 11:3 affirms, *"Through faith we understand that the worlds were framed by the word of God, so that what is seen was not made out of things which are visible."* Long before quarks and gluons were named, this ancient text pointed to a profound truth: that the visible world emerges from the invisible. Modern science confirms this notion with startling precision. What appears to be solid is mostly empty space. What seems still is in constant motion. What we call "matter" is, at its core, organized energy held together by forces that cannot be seen, only measured and inferred.

This chapter invites the reader to enter this invisible world, not to abandon faith for science or science for faith, but to stand at the crossroads where both converge. For in the deep structure of the universe, hidden beneath the veil of appearances, we may find not only the fingerprints of physics, but the whisper of God.

II. The Blueprint Beneath Reality

For centuries, humans believed the universe was made of solid things: earth, stone, fire, flesh. But as our tools grew sharper and our questions deeper, that illusion dissolved. We discovered that what we call matter is mostly emptiness, and what seems stable is born from ceaseless motion. At the edge of our understanding stands a towering achievement: the Standard Model of Particle Physics. Not a structure of steel and stone, but a map of invisible interactions, a catalogue of particles and forces so precise that it can predict the behavior of reality itself to more than a dozen decimal places. It does not merely describe the universe, it deciphers it.

At the core of this model are fundamental particles, not the bricks of the universe, but something stranger: its alphabet. There are quarks, the restless elements that bind together in trios to form protons and neutrons. There are leptons, which include the ghost-like neutrino and the well-known electron, so small, so light, they dance through matter undetected. And then there are the bosons, the messengers, the carriers of force, photons that deliver light, gluons that bind nuclei, and W and Z bosons that govern the weak interactions in radioactive decay.

All of this would still float unmoored, weightless, meaningless, if not for the Higgs boson and its invisible partner, the Higgs field. Long theorized and finally discovered in 2012, the Higgs boson is not just another particle. It is the evidence of a deeper sea in which all others swim. As particles move through the Higgs field, they gain mass, not because mass is added like weight on a scale, but because resistance is created, like a hand pushing through water. Without it, there would be no stars, no atoms, no life. Without the Higgs, there is only chaos, light-speed dust in a void.

The Standard Model is a masterwork, elegant, precise, predictive. Yet it is incomplete. It cannot explain gravity. It cannot account for dark matter or dark energy. And so, the mystery deepens.

In our most advanced understanding of physics, particles are not things. They are not marbles or points or dots of matter floating in space. They are excitations in underlying quantum fields, vibrations in the fabric of reality itself. Imagine a calm ocean; toss in a stone, and ripples spread. Now imagine that ocean exists everywhere and that each type of particle is a ripple in a different kind of ocean, a quantum field.

In this view, reality is not made of particles, but of fields, layered one upon another like overlapping songs. The electron is a tremor in the electron field. The photon is a disturbance in the electromagnetic field. And in the empty space between stars, where we might presume nothing exists, vacuum energy boils with activity. Space is not empty. It seethes. It fluctuates. Virtual particles blink in and out of existence like fireflies in a storm, a restless ocean of potential.

This is the quantum vacuum, an eerie silence that hums with hidden music, where "nothing" is more alive than anything we can see. The ancient scriptures declared, *"What is seen was not made out of what is visible."* Modern physics now speaks that truth, with equations and accelerators confirming it: the visible arises from the invisible.

As we descend into these unseen realms, we do not find chaos, we find order, symmetry, and beauty beyond reckoning. The laws that govern these particles are not arbitrary; they obey strict, mathematical rules known as group theory, a language of symmetry, rotation, and transformation. Like snowflakes forming from water vapor, the universe crystallizes from patterns, governed by symmetry groups like SU(3), SU(2), and U(1), strange names for astonishing laws.

Symmetry is not decoration. It is the law of being. When physicists probe the Standard Model, they find a kind of hidden perfection, a balance that shapes the very identity of each particle and force. And yet, in the breaking of that symmetry, like the breaking of dawn from night: mass, structure, and diversity emerge. Creation is not the collapse of order into chaos, but the transformation of perfect symmetry into rich complexity.

Some physicists go further still. They dream of supersymmetry, a mirror world where every particle has a hidden twin. Others explore string theory, where particles are not points but tiny, vibrating strings, each note a different particle, each frequency a new dimension. In this theory, reality is a symphony. The universe is music played on a multidimensional harp, perhaps strummed by the fingers of God.

"Through faith we understand that the worlds were framed by the word of God..." (Hebrews 11:3).

And now, through science, we glimpse how that word may still represent itself in every quark and quantum wave, in every unseen symmetry and unbroken field.

The invisible is not empty. It is the birthplace of all that is.

III. The Genesis of Matter

Before the stars, before galaxies, before the whisper of wind or the beat of a human heart, there was nothing. No time. No space. No form. Then, in an instant that defies comprehension, everything ignited.

This is the great cosmic dawn we call the Big Bang. Not an explosion in space, but an explosion of space itself, a birth cry of reality. At Time = 0, all the energy that would become galaxies, oceans, minds, and music was compressed into a point smaller than an atom. It was a moment governed not by logic, but by paradox, a domain called the Planck epoch, where the known laws of physics collapse into mystery.

And then, light.

As the universe expanded, time began its relentless march. Energy cooled, and from pure fire emerged the first particles, quarks and electrons, fleeting and volatile. Yet for every particle that burst into being, its shadow-self, antimatter, appeared beside it. They should have annihilated one another entirely, canceling out the possibility of anything at all. But they didn't. For reasons still not fully understood, there was a slight imbalance, a divine tipping of the scales called baryogenesis, that left a remnant of matter behind. That remnant is everything we are.

Moments later came nucleosynthesis, when the first atomic nuclei, hydrogen, helium, a touch of lithium, were forged in the searing heat. The building blocks of stars and life were formed not in the cradle of galaxies, but in the furnace of a newborn cosmos, less than twenty minutes old.

And yet, the universe was not merely created. It was calibrated.

Had the cosmological constant been slightly stronger, the universe would have torn itself apart. Had it been weaker, gravity would have crushed all matter back into a singularity. The fine-structure constant, which determines the strength of electromagnetic interaction, is tuned with such precision that even the slightest variation would make atoms, and life, impossible. The odds are astronomical, absurd even. Some physicists call it luck. Others invoke the anthropic principle: that we observe this universe because it's the one that permits our observation.

But some see something deeper.

They see design, not imposed from outside, but woven into the very equations of being. They see a Creator not only speaking light into existence, but whispering constants, scripting the laws of physics with such exactitude that matter itself could arise, cool, clump, and one day contemplate its own beginnings.

This is not just cosmology. It is a modern representation of Genesis.

IV. The Logos and Quantum Strangeness

There is a silent order behind the chaos, a hidden rhythm that governs the dance of galaxies and the spin of electrons. It is not merely that the universe behaves. It is that the universe obeys. And even more mysteriously, it obeys laws we can understand.

This is one of the most staggering truths in all of science: the cosmos is intelligible.

Why should this be so? Why should a creature made of dust and water be able to comprehend the inner workings of stars, to write equations that describe black holes, to simulate the birth of the universe itself? Why should reality be written in the language of mathematics, a language we did not invent, but discovered, like explorers stumbling upon a code etched into the structure of existence?

Physicist Eugene Wigner once called this the "unreasonable effectiveness of mathematics in the natural sciences." He marveled that abstract mathematical formulations, devised in the quiet of human minds, should so effortlessly describe the behavior of quarks, fields, and cosmic expansion. It is not simply useful. It is astonishing, as if the universe were built not of random accidents, but of intended logic.

Long before quantum fields and spacetime curvature, the Apostle John gave this order a name: Logos.

"In the beginning was the Word (Logos), and the Word was with God, and the Word was God. Through Him all things were made." *(John 1:1–3)*

The Greek *Logos* means more than "word." It means reason, pattern, logic, the rational structure of all things. And in Christian theology, the Logos is not an idea but a Person: Christ, the mind behind matter, the One through whom reality coheres.

This is not metaphor. It is metaphysics.

To the Christian physicist, every discovery, every symmetrical law, every constant, every field equation, is not a detour from faith, but a glimpse into the mind of God. Physics becomes not just a tool of inquiry, but an act of worship. In the harmony of equations, in the coherence of laws that span billions of light-years, we find the fingerprints of a Logos that does not just explain the universe, but sustains it.

In a cosmos governed by Logos, science is not the enemy of faith. It is the answer of it.

***

There are also places in science where the human mind begins to tremble, not from fear, but from awe. Quantum entanglement is one of those places.

Imagine two particles born together in the same moment, perhaps in the firestorm of a dying star or the controlled violence of a laboratory collision. Once linked, they drift apart, miles, even light-years, but they remain inexplicably connected. Alter the state of one, and the other changes instantly, as if distance were an illusion. As if time had no authority. As if reality itself had a pulse that beats beneath space.

This is entanglement. Einstein called it "spooky action at a distance." To this day, no one fully understands it. But its effects are real, measurable, undeniable. Entangled particles defy the speed limit of light. They refuse to conform to classical logic. They whisper of a reality that is nonlocal, where separateness is an illusion and connection is the deeper truth.

Quantum mechanics shattered the old Newtonian world of predictability. In the classical view, objects had location and momentum, clear trajectories and separable existences. But the quantum realm offers no such comfort. Here, particles exist in superpositions, in multiple states at once. They are waves of probability until measured. They flicker between realities like whispers in a storm.

The Heisenberg Uncertainty Principle tells us that we cannot know both the position and momentum of a particle with absolute precision. This is not because we lack tools; it is because reality itself resists precision. Reality is relational, dynamic, shimmering.

And then comes Bell's Theorem, the dagger in the heart of classical locality. Bell proved, with mathematical rigor, that no local hidden variables, no secret, deterministic mechanism within the particles, could explain the correlations seen in entangled systems. The world is not only strange. It is irreducibly interconnected.

Experiments have confirmed it time and again. A measurement here can affect a result there, instantly, without signal or force. Something deeper than space is at work.

For centuries, Christian theology has affirmed that God is omnipresent, not stretched thin like a mist, but fully present everywhere. He is not bound by space or time, but sustains them. He is near to the brokenhearted (Psalm 34:18), and at the same moment, enthroned beyond the stars (Isaiah 66:1).

In quantum entanglement, we glimpse an analogy. Not a proof, but a resonance. Just as two entangled particles defy distance and remain mysteriously united, so the Creator is intimately connected to every quark and galaxy. There is no "place" God must travel to be near. There is no moment He does not already inhabit.

The quantum world whispers something the Christian faith has long declared: presence is not confined by proximity.

"Where shall I go from your Spirit? Or where shall I flee from your presence?"

(Psalm 139:7)

God's omnipresence is not merely spatial. It is relational. He is not just *everywhere*, He is *with* us, intricately, specifically,

66

personally. Just as a particle seems to "know" what has happened to its twin across the void, so God knows, without delay, without absence, the thoughts of every heart, the fall of every sparrow, the wound of every soul.

Quantum mechanics forces us to reconsider our assumptions about separateness. Christianity has always done the same. The Incarnation, the idea that God became man without ceasing to be infinite, is the ultimate declaration that distance between heaven and earth is not a barrier. That the eternal can enter time without being diminished.

In quantum entanglement, we find a physical mirror image of the spiritual unity of creation. Paul writes in Colossians that "in Him all things hold together" (Col. 1:17). This is not poetry, it is metaphysics. Christ is not merely a historical figure, but the sustaining principle of the cosmos, the Logos in whom quantum fields, gravitational curvature, and electromagnetic waves all find their coherence.

Just as entangled particles cannot be considered in isolation, so no soul exists apart from the divine presence that holds them. There is no part of you, no cell, no tear, no synapse, that is unknown or unreachable to God. The entanglement we observe in physics becomes a metaphor for the Creator's intimate nearness to all things.

Bell's Theorem does more than dismantle classical assumptions; it dismantles the idea of a clockwork universe, wound up and left to tick. It strikes at Deism, the belief that God may exist but is absent, uninvolved. The quantum world says otherwise. Reality is not mechanistic. It is interactive, responsive, uncertain but relational.

The God of Scripture is not a watchmaker. He is a shepherd, a Father, a presence that pervades and sustains. Quantum physics does not prove this, but it removes the philosophical barriers that once made such a belief seem implausible.

If the world is not deterministic... if particles are shaped by observation... if nothing exists truly alone... then the idea of a present, active, sustaining God is no longer irrational. It becomes the best explanation for why rationality, coherence, and presence exist at all.

Some scientists recoil at these theological parallels. They accuse believers of inserting God into gaps in our understanding. But this is not a God of the gaps. This is a God of the whole, the Logos who is not the explanation for what we do not know, but the reason anything can be known.

Mystery is not ignorance. Mystery is the space where reason bows to awe. And quantum mechanics, more than any other field, has taught physicists to kneel again.

There is humility in not understanding. There is reverence in acknowledging that reality is deeper than measurement. And there is worship in realizing that the closer science peers into the fabric of the cosmos, the more it begins to resemble something... personal.

Quantum entanglement reminds us that we live in a connected universe, one where distance is not disconnection, and time is not a barrier to presence. This is the language of both physics and faith. It is the song of a cosmos created not by randomness but by relationship.

So let us no longer be surprised that science and faith find harmony. In the entangled particles and collapsing wavefunctions, in the weird and wondrous laws of the unseen, we hear tunes of a truth older than atoms:

"I am with you always, even to the end of the age." *(Matthew 28:20)*

Not confined. Not absent. But entangled in the deepest sense, not just across space, but with our very being.

V. The Cross and the Quark

There is a hidden rhythm to reality, a cosmic choreography of life, death, and renewal. It pulses through galaxies and genes, through dying stars and falling leaves. And it is written into the smallest particles of matter. Physics and faith, it turns out, tell a parallel story: that everything which dies is not lost, but transformed.

We begin not with philosophy, but with the fundamental stuff of the universe. Quarks, the building blocks of protons and neutrons, are never seen alone. They are forever bound, forever interacting, held together by the strongest force in the cosmos, the strong nuclear force. On their own, they cannot exist. Only in relationship do they take form. Only in bonding do they become what we recognize as matter.

This is not just physical truth. It is spiritual resonance.

"In Him all things hold together."

(Colossians 1:17)

This single verse from the Apostle Paul holds both the mystery of the Incarnation and the mystery of the atom. Matter is not self-sustaining. It is not inert. It is sustained, moment by moment, by the Word who spoke the cosmos into being. Beneath every proton lies a whisper of divine will: "Be." And it is.

Yet this sustained being is not static. It decays. It transforms. It dies.

Take beta decay, a process that occurs when a neutron transforms into a proton, emitting an electron and a ghostly neutrino. It is a violent, invisible sacrifice, a moment where identity is shattered and reshaped. What was once one thing becomes another. And out of that change, life continues.

Even here, in the quiet decay of subatomic particles, we find a mirror of the Cross.

At Calvary, God entered matter, not merely as an observer but as one of us, subject to entropy, suffering, and death. The Creator, in whom all things hold together, allowed Himself to be torn apart. And in that breaking, something new emerged: resurrection. Not just the reanimation of flesh, but the inauguration of a new kind of reality.

In physics, this is showed in symmetry breaking. In the early universe, perfect symmetry reigned, a formless, high-energy unity. But then, symmetry broke. Forces separated. Phase transitions birthed the particles and interactions that would form atoms, stars, and eventually, sentient life. The breaking was not destruction. It was creation.

So too, the broken body of Christ is not the end, it is the beginning of new creation.

In Christian liturgy, we do not merely remember this transformation, we partake in it. The Eucharist is a staggering claim: that matter, bread and wine, can become the real presence of Christ. Not symbolically alone, but truly, mysteriously, sacramentally.

Modern physics tells us that matter is not what it seems. A piece of bread is mostly empty space, held together by quantum forces and fields. It is not solid. It is vibrating energy, shaped by information, rooted in unseen laws. If all matter is sustained by something deeper than itself, then perhaps it is not so strange that the Creator can enter it, again and again.

The Eucharist is not a denial of science. It is its fulfillment. It is the claim that the God who created quarks and phase transitions can still speak into matter and say, "This is my body."

To the materialist, this sounds absurd. But quantum mechanics has taught us to be wary of surface appearances. Particles are waves. Observation changes outcomes. Location is uncertain. Reality is participatory. And so perhaps, just perhaps, the same Christ who conquered death can enter bread, not figuratively, but fundamentally.

Physics does not preach sermons. But it tells stories of transformation, of decay, of rebirth.

A white dwarf collapses. Its atoms are crushed, its electrons stripped. It dies and becomes a neutron star, denser than anything the human mind can comprehend.

A photon, massless and invisible, collides with an atom, and gives birth to matter and antimatter.

A collapsing star explodes in a supernova, seeding galaxies with the elements of life: iron for our blood, calcium for our bones.

In each case, death is not the end. It is the threshold. The place where old forms are broken and new realities emerge.

The same is true of resurrection. Not the survival of the soul alone, but the transformation of the body, of the cosmos itself. Paul speaks of a "spiritual body" not less physical, but more real, more alive, free from corruption (1 Cor. 15:42–44).

Resurrection is not escape from matter. It is the redemption of matter.

What if the physics of the universe has always hinted at this? What if every decay, every phase transition, every supernova is a parable, preparing us to believe that death is not the final word?

The Cross is not merely a moment in time, it is a structure in the heart of reality. It reveals that sacrifice is not defeat but transformation. It reveals that matter itself was made for more than entropy. It was made for glory.

In the structure of particles and the decay of atoms, in the mystery of mass and the resurrection of the dead, we find one great theme:

That all things are being remade.

"Behold, I make all things new." *(Revelation 21:5)*

And so we stand at the edge of science and faith, with quarks in one hand and the Eucharist in the other, and we declare:

The universe is not mute.

It speaks of a Cross.

It speaks of a tomb.

It speaks of a table.

And it speaks of a dawn

when matter shall rise, and death shall die.

VI. The God Particle? Revisiting the Higgs Boson

It was July 4th, 2012, when physicists at CERN stepped before the world and declared that they had found it. After nearly half a century of searching, the elusive Higgs boson, nicknamed by some "the God Particle" had finally shown itself in the shudder of subatomic collisions. It was a moment that electrified science. Headlines screamed of divine discovery. And yet, beneath the fireworks of media frenzy, something far more profound had taken place.

No gods had been discovered. No temples shaken. And yet... the very fabric of reality had spoken.

What they had truly found was not God, but a ghost, a fleeting relic of the Higgs field, the invisible energy that quietly weaves through the entire universe, granting mass to the massless, form to the formless, substance to the otherwise weightless quantum world.

Without it, there would be no stars, no gravity, no galaxies, no you. Without it, matter would drift like mist, structureless, anchorless, meaningless.

And this is why the Higgs boson matters. Not because it is divine. But because it reveals how delicate, how tuned, how astonishingly graced our reality really is.

In the Standard Model of particle physics, particles acquire mass not by nature, but through interaction. The Higgs field, an invisible ocean of energy that permeates all of space, resists the motion of certain particles, slowing them down, granting them mass. Like swimmers moving through molasses, some particles are caught, others slip through. This cosmic resistance shapes everything.

Photons, for example, pass through the Higgs field untouched. That's why light is massless and can streak across the cosmos at the speed limit of reality. But the W and Z bosons, carriers of the weak nuclear force, wade heavily through the field. That's why they are massive, and why the weak force is weak: it doesn't travel far.

This simple interaction, field meets particle, is the silent engine of cosmic structure. It is what allows electrons to orbit, atoms to bond, stars to burn. The Higgs field is the scaffold of material being.

But it is more than a mechanism. It is a metaphor.

Like the Higgs field, grace is invisible. It does not shout or shine. It moves beneath, through, and within. It gives weight to our lives, coherence to our stories, strength to our weakness. It is not a force in the classical sense. It does not compel, it enables.

"In Him we live and move and have our being."

(Acts 17:28)

What is the Higgs field, if not a shadow of this truth? A field that holds all together, without being seen. A presence that sustains mass, without being mass itself. It is not the Holy Spirit, but it might be the physics of a world touched by Spirit.

And what of the Higgs boson, the so-called "God Particle"? Its nickname, while thrilling to journalists, is a theological misstep. Coined half-seriously by physicist Leon Lederman (who originally wanted to call it "the goddamn particle" for its elusiveness), the label stuck, but misleads. The boson is not divine. It does not create. It does not sustain. It is a signal, a footprint in the quantum snow, that the Higgs field is real.

To deify the boson is to confuse the messenger with the message, the veil with the face, the whisper with the Word.

There is something haunting about the Higgs field. It exists at a constant value, roughly 246 GeV across the cosmos. Why this value? Why this interaction strength? A small shift would make atoms impossible, stars unformed, life unthinkable. It is not just that the Higgs field works, it is that it works so precisely, as if reality has been tuned for meaning.

Some physicists appeal to the anthropic principle: we observe these conditions because only in such a universe could observers like us exist. But theology dares to ask a deeper question: *Why should there be any observers at all? Why should there be a field that gifts mass, a universe that forms stars, a world that can speak of grace and wonder and God?*

In this way, the Higgs field is not the divine itself, but a signpost, a pointer to a reality where the material and the spiritual are not at war, but aligned. A world where the unseen is more foundational than the seen.

It would be easy, and lazy, to draw simple equations:

Higgs = God.

Boson = Holy Spirit.

Field = Grace.

But the truth is subtler, more beautiful. Physics cannot prove God. But it can describe a universe open to God, a universe where unseen things shape all that is seen, where invisible fields govern stars, and where fleeting bosons hint at depths yet unexplored.

Theologians speak of the Holy Spirit as the one who gives life, who binds all in unity, who animates the church and the cosmos alike. Not seen, but felt. Not possessed, but present. The Higgs field, too, is not seen. But its effects are everywhere. It is the gentle architect of structure, the quiet breath of the material order.

In this sense, we might say: God is not the Higgs. But the Higgs reminds us of how God works.

Not by domination, but by presence.

Not by coercion, but by sustaining.

Not with spectacle, but with subtlety.

In a universe of astonishing particles and precise laws, perhaps the most astonishing truth is this: that something as silent as a field, as fleeting as a boson, can hold together the architecture of being.

The Higgs boson is not God, but it reminds us that the deepest truths are often invisible. That the real foundations of reality are not what we see, but what we cannot see. And that, in the very heart of matter, we find a whisper:

"Let there be mass. Let there be form. Let there be meaning."

And there was.

VII. The Image of God and the Observer Principle

In the strange world of quantum mechanics, observation is not a passive act. It is an event. A turning point. A moment of creation.

Before a quantum system is measured, it exists in a cloud of probabilities, a ghostly superposition of all possible outcomes. The electron is not here or there. The photon has not yet chosen wave or particle. Reality hovers, undecided. But when the observer steps in, when a mind looks, measures, perceives, the wavefunction collapses, and the world decides.

This is the observer effect: the notion that reality, at its most fundamental level, responds to the act of observation. It is a notion both thrilling and unsettling, and for many, it begs a staggering question: *Is consciousness somehow built into the fabric of the universe?*

In the laboratories of physics, particles flicker between states as if awaiting a witness. In the pages of theology, humanity is described not as an accident of dust and time, but as Imago Dei, the image of God. What if these are not contradictions, but confirmations? What if the participatory nature of quantum reality reflects a deeper truth: that the cosmos was made to be known?

"And God said, Let us make man in our image, after our likeness..."

(Genesis 1:26)

What does it mean to be made in the image of the Creator? Certainly not in form. God is not bound by flesh or limit. But in mind, in spirit, in the capacity to see, to know, to speak meaning into chaos, we reflect the Divine. We are not detached spectators. We are co-creators of comprehension, perceiving the universe not from the outside, but as intimate participants.

This is not New Age mysticism. It is a fundamental truth hinted in the most advanced corners of physics: that reality is not wholly real until it is observed. And yet who, before stars, before humans, before photons met eye or sensor, who observed?

God.

Not as a being among beings, but as Being itself. The eternal Observer. The ultimate consciousness who does not merely measure, but sustains.

"He is before all things, and in Him all things hold together."

(Colossians 1:17)

If the quantum world waits for a mind to fix its state, then perhaps existence itself waits for the Divine Mind, the cosmic Observer who calls reality not into randomness, but into order, continuity, and purpose. In this view, consciousness is not an emergent glitch of matter, it is foundational. A shadow of the One who sees all.

And we, fragile, fleeting observers, are invited into this act. Every time we gaze at the stars, decode the atom, map the genome, or imagine what lies beyond the horizon, we participate in a sacred tradition: the act of knowing as worship, of perception as communion.

To observe, then, is to recollect the original act of creation: "Let there be…"

And there was.

In sum, particle physics, to some, seems cold. Mechanistic. Sterile. The whir of accelerators. The collision of invisible shards. The enumeration of spin, charge, mass.

But to others, it is nothing less than a modern hymn.

Each boson and baryon, each symmetry broken and law upheld, is a verse in a grand cosmic liturgy. The language of quarks and leptons is not a rival to faith, but a dialect of awe.

Once, we feared that the microscope would displace the soul, that science would erase the sacred. But now, we know better. We see that the closer we look, the more mysterious the world becomes. And mystery is the shared cathedral of both physicist and theologian.

The Higgs field whispers of hidden grace. Entanglement suggest divine presence. The observer principle gestures toward a mind that underlies the world. Even the decay of particles hints at death and resurrection, transformation and transcendence.

This is not poetic license. It is the poetry within the license of reality itself.

"The heavens declare the glory of God; the skies proclaim the work of his hands."

(Psalm 19:1)

But not only the skies. The subatomic world declares it too. The vacuum fluctuations and virtual particles. The mathematical symmetries so precise they feel sung rather than solved. The constants so fine-tuned they seem chosen. In all of it, we are beckoned to wonder, not as children scared by mystery, but as beings called by it.

There is room here for faith. There is room here for science. For in truth, they are not two voices, but **two ears of the same mind**, together, listening to the sacred hum of existence.

From the particle to the prophet, from the quantum field to the fields of Galilee, we are surrounded by revelation. Not always loud. Rarely simple. But always pulsing with **meaning**.

The atom has spoken, so have the scriptures.

And the heart still whispers: *"This is holy ground."*

Reflective Questions

If everything in the universe is made from invisible particles held together by unseen forces, how does that shape your understanding of faith in what you cannot see but believe is real?

_____

_____

_____

_____

What does the discovery of order and symmetry in the subatomic world reveal to you about the nature of God as both Creator and Sustainer?

_____

_____

_____

_____

How do concepts like quantum uncertainty or entanglement challenge, or deepen, your perception of divine mystery and interconnectedness in creation?

_____

_____

_____

_____

Chapter 4
The Laws of Order

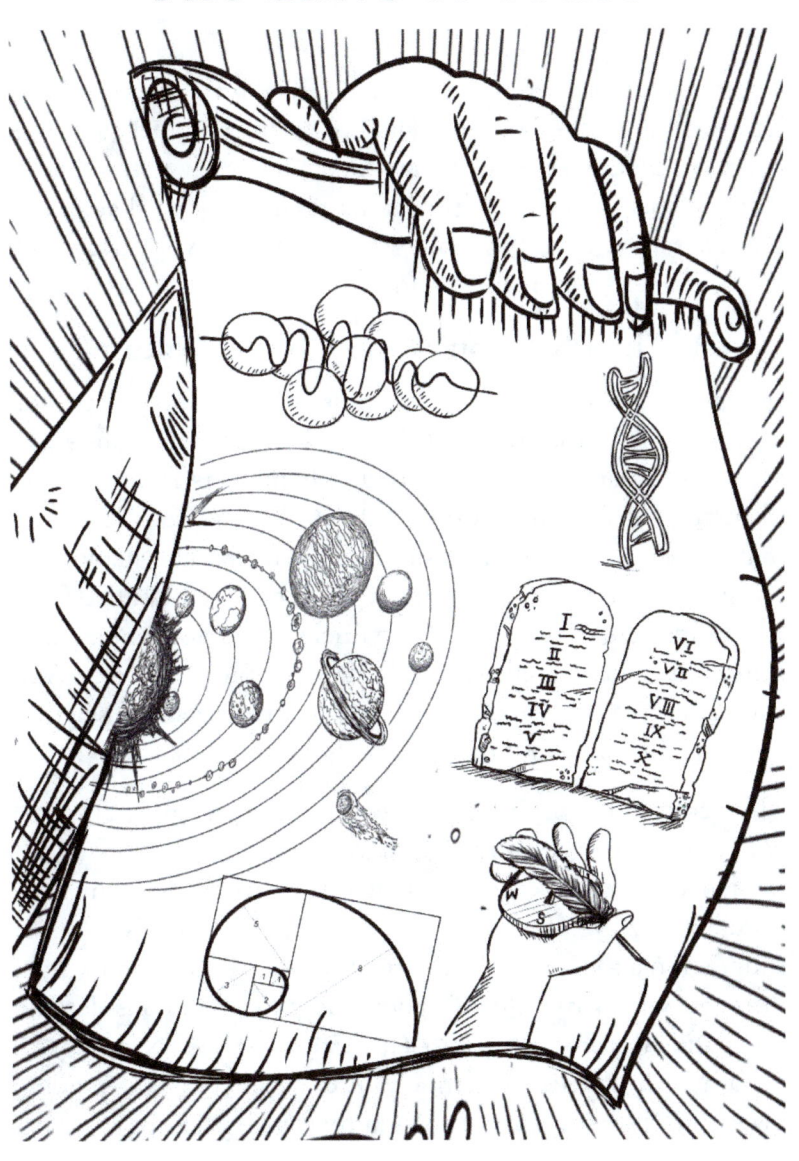

For ages, they've stood like distant stars, science and faith, one gazing through a lens of proof, the other through a window of belief. However, their distance is often only imagined. What if the laws that govern the cosmos are not barriers to faith, but verses in its sacred song?

To the soul attuned, science is no rival to God; it is His handwriting in the heavens, His breath in the blueprint. The order of the universe, so finely tuned, so fiercely precise, does not whisper chance; it proclaims design. Not chaos, but choreography. Not void, but voice. And in every orbit and atom, a quiet song of the Divine.

I. The Precision of the Laws of Nature

It begins with precision, an exactness so profound it demands not only intellectual acknowledgment but reverent wonder. In a universe spanning some 93 billion light-years in observable diameter, filled with an estimated 2 trillion galaxies, the laws that govern its every motion remain uncannily stable and consistent. These are not arbitrary rules, nor do they arise from chaos. Instead, they resemble the finely-tuned notes of a grand symphony, one that evokes not confusion, but coherence. And for many, that coherence points beyond the veil of science, reaching into the heart of divinity.

The constants of nature are not simply mathematical curiosities. They are the immutable scaffolding upon which existence rests. Take, for instance, the speed of light in a vacuum, 299,792,458 meters per second. This value is not only foundational to Einstein's theory of relativity but is intertwined into the very structure of space and time. Or consider the gravitational constant, $G = 6.67430 \times 10^{-11}$ N(m/kg)^2, dictating the force of attraction between masses, guiding planets in their orbits, and stars in their life cycles.

Slight alterations to these constants would yield a vastly different, likely uninhabitable universe. If the gravitational constant were even a fraction stronger, stars would burn out too quickly for life to evolve. If it were weaker, matter might never have coalesced into stars and galaxies. Likewise, the fine-structure constant, governing electromagnetic interaction, must remain within a razor-thin margin to permit the formation of atoms, the chemical basis of life.

This remarkable fine-tuning has led to what physicists call the "anthropic principle": the idea that the universe appears to be designed in such a way as to support life. There are two broad versions of this principle. The "weak" anthropic principle simply states that we must observe a universe capable of supporting observers. The "strong" version posits that the universe must have properties that allow life to develop at some point. Yet neither version explains *why* the constants are as they are.

Modern cosmology has introduced ideas like the multiverse to account for this fine-tuning, suggesting an infinite number of universes with varying physical laws, and we just happen to live in one where conditions permit life. While intellectually intriguing, such hypotheses remain beyond empirical testing, making them metaphysical assertions cloaked in scientific language. They may answer the "how" but not the "why."

The Apostle Paul, writing centuries before the advent of physics, put it this way: "For since the creation of the world God's invisible qualities, His eternal power and divine nature, have been clearly seen, being understood from what has been made" (Romans 1:20). In that verse lies the profound insight that what we observe in nature, its precision, beauty, and order, are not mere coincidences, but manifestations of the divine.

Why is the universe intelligible? Why does it yield its secrets to mathematics? Nobel Prize-winning physicist Eugene Wigner pondered this in his famous essay, *The Unreasonable Effectiveness of Mathematics in the Natural Sciences.* He marveled that abstract mathematical constructs, developed in human minds, so accurately describe the physical world. There is no necessity that mathematics should work, and yet it does, often with uncanny precision.

The laws of physics, whether Newtonian mechanics, quantum field theory, or general relativity, are expressed in mathematical language. Gravity is described by Einstein's elegant field equations; quantum interactions are encapsulated in Schrödinger's wave function. These are not chaotic musings but articulate descriptions of phenomena that span both the vast and the minute. Why should particles follow probabilistic rules encoded in a complex-valued wave function? Why should light curve around massive objects exactly as general relativity predicts?

Christian theology has long supported the idea of a lawful universe. The biblical understanding of God is of a rational, consistent Creator. The Book of Genesis opens with a God who brings order to chaos, separating light from darkness, water from land, day from night. The refrain "And God saw that it was good" repeats like a poetic affirmation of order. In this narrative, creation is not an arbitrary act but a deliberate structuring.

Historically, many founders of modern science were themselves men of deep faith. Johannes Kepler, who discovered the laws of planetary motion, viewed his work as uncovering God's geometric plan for the cosmos. Isaac Newton, whose laws of motion and gravity still serve as the bedrock of classical mechanics, wrote more about theology than physics. Faraday, Maxwell, and Pascal likewise integrated scientific inquiry with theological reverence.

The predictability we find in the laws of nature implies reliability, a trait we typically associate with intelligence and intention. If physical laws were capricious, science would be impossible. We would be unable to build technology, predict outcomes, or even survive. The very act of conducting an experiment rests on the assumption that the universe will behave tomorrow as it did today.

Further still, the concept of symmetry lies at the heart of modern physics. Noether's theorem, a profound result in theoretical physics, connects symmetries with conservation laws: time symmetry implies conservation of energy, space symmetry implies conservation of momentum. These deep correspondences reveal an internal elegance in the architecture of reality.

String theory, an ambitious attempt to unify all fundamental forces of nature, posits that the basic building blocks of matter are not point particles but vibrating one-dimensional strings. These strings are unimaginably small, about 10^{-35} meters in length, and their vibrational states determine the properties of particles. What we perceive as electrons, quarks, or photons are simply different modes of vibration of the same fundamental string.

String theory operates in a universe that includes up to 11 dimensions, most of which are compactified or curled up at scales far smaller than can be observed. These extra dimensions are crucial for the mathematical consistency of the theory. The equations of string theory elegantly reproduce known particle behaviors and offer potential explanations for phenomena like gravity's relative weakness compared to other forces.

One of the most fascinating aspects of string theory is its requirement for supersymmetry that is a theoretical symmetry between particles of matter and force-carrying particles. Though supersymmetric partners have yet to be observed, the idea has inspired entire fields of research and continues to shape our understanding of particle physics.

Perhaps most striking is the way string theory naturally accommodates gravity, something other quantum theories struggle to do. Gravity emerges not as an imposed force, but as a consequence of the geometry of spacetime within the framework of string interactions. This makes string theory a candidate for the long-sought theory of everything, one that unifies general relativity and quantum mechanics.

Some theologians and philosophers find in string theory a poetic echo of divine creativity. The universe, built from vibrating strings, resembles a cosmic instrument played by a divine musician. Just as the vibrations of violin strings create harmonies, so too do these fundamental strings generate the symphony of particles and forces. In this view, the music of the cosmos is not random noise but a carefully composed melody.

Cosmologist Paul Davies once remarked, "Science can proceed only if the scientist adopts an essentially theological worldview." This is not to argue for dogma in the laboratory, but to acknowledge that the foundational assumptions of science, including order, intelligibility, consistency are themselves faith-based premises. They cannot be proven by science, but are necessary for science to operate.

To a believer, the precision of nature is not a riddle but a revelation. The constants and equations are the language of God, spoken across time and space. As Psalm 19:1 declares,

"The heavens declare the glory of God; the skies proclaim the work of His hands."

The awe inspired by the fine-tuning of the cosmos is not an argument from ignorance but an argument from wonder. It is not a retreat from reason but its fulfillment. The deeper we probe into the mechanics of reality, the more we encounter a kind of divine resonance, a sacred architecture whose very stability invites both scientific inquiry and spiritual reflection.

Ultimately, the harmony of the physical universe beckons us toward a greater truth: that behind every constant, every equation, and every law lies not just a principle, but a Person. Not merely a force, but a Father.

And that changes everything.

II. The Laws of Thermodynamics A.K.A. The Order of Energy and Life

There is a rhythm to existence, an invisible cadence undergirding everything from the burning of stars to the flicker of a candle. The laws of thermodynamics, though born of physics and chemistry, are not sterile formulae carved onto chalkboards. They are revelations of how creation is structured, how energy pulses through time, and how decay is not the end of the story but the beginning of deeper questions. When viewed through the lens of faith, these laws, particularly the second law, with its relentless march of entropy, trace not hopelessness, but harmony: a sacred balance between freedom and order, decay and renewal, science and spirit.

The **First Law of Thermodynamics,** also known as the law of energy conservation, declares that energy cannot be created or destroyed in an isolated system; it can only change forms. The total amount remains constant.

At first glance, this is a simple mechanical principle: a gas heats, a piston moves, a machine runs. But behind the physics lies a profound metaphysical truth: **nothing is wasted**. All energy, whether light, heat, or motion, endures. It is transformed, redirected, and reimagined, but never vanishes.

Faith finds a beautiful resonance here. The constancy of energy mirrors the constancy of God, unchanging, ever-present, not subject to the whims of chaos. In Scripture, the divine is described as the Alpha and Omega, the One "in whom there is no shadow of turning" (James 1:17). Just as the universe obeys this deep conservation, so too does the spiritual life affirm that no suffering is in vain, no act of love disappears into nothingness. All things are accounted for. All things endure in some form, either as energy in the universe or as spiritual consequence in eternity.

To the faithful, the First Law is more than science; it is **assurance**. The God who orders the cosmos is not absent, and what He has set in motion He sustains with unfailing precision.

The **Second Law of Thermodynamics** states that in any energy transfer or transformation, the total entropy of a closed system will increase over time. Put simply, **disorder increases**. Systems tend toward decay. Heat disperses. Organization degrades. Time has a direction, from order to chaos.

It is a law that explains so much of our reality: why buildings crumble, why bodies age, why stars die. In a purely material sense, it suggests a tragic undertone: all things wind down. The arrow of time points not to permanence, but to dissolution.

And yet, this law, as cold as it may sound, has overtones with spiritual depth, for it aligns with what the Christian tradition has long understood as the Fall: the entry of disorder, sin, and suffering into a once-perfect world. In Genesis, harmony gives way to rupture. The garden becomes wilderness. Relationship gives way to separation. The second law can be seen as the physical parallel of that spiritual event.

But faith does not leave entropy as the final word. The arc of Scripture, and indeed the arc of hope, is that what is broken can be redeemed. Decay is not the end; it is the soil from which resurrection grows. In the natural world, we see glimpses of this: compost becomes nourishment, forest fires clear the way for new growth, stars collapse and give birth to new galaxies.

Entropy may govern systems, but it **does not govern grace**.

In Romans 8:21, Paul writes of the creation itself "groaning as in the pains of childbirth," waiting to be liberated from its bondage to decay. This is thermodynamics spoken in spiritual terms. The universe yearns. And faith answers that yearning not with denial, but with promise.

The **Third Law of Thermodynamics** asserts that as a system approaches absolute zero, the lowest possible temperature, its entropy approaches a constant minimum. In this frozen stillness, all disorder ceases. Motion halts. Everything settles into its final, most orderly state.

There's something haunting and holy about this idea: that there exists, theoretically, a condition of complete calm, complete stillness, a resting point from which no more chaos can emerge. The laws of the universe themselves anticipate an end to disorder.

Faith recognizes this yearning for rest. The idea of **Sabbath**, a day of rest, is more than a religious observance. It is a spiritual memory of a cosmic principle. The soul, like the universe, longs for stillness, for peace, for restoration. "Be still, and know that I am God," the psalmist writes (Psalm 46:10). The

Third Law, in its abstract way, gestures toward that stillness, the end of striving, the peace that transcends disorder.

The final rest of creation is not annihilation, but **completion**.

The harmony between thermodynamics and theology lies in the ability of both to describe reality without contradiction. One speaks the language of energy and entropy; the other speaks of hope, redemption, and eternal truth. But both point toward something coherent, something structured, something that invites reverence.

Thermodynamics reminds us of our limits: that we are mortal, that systems decay, that energy dissipates. Faith does not deny these realities; it embraces them, yet insists that beyond the limits lies promise.

Entropy may describe the journey, but it is not the destination.

Even science recognizes its own boundaries. The laws of thermodynamics, though powerful, cannot explain *why* the universe exists, *why* these laws govern it, or *why* there is order instead of chaos. Those are questions of meaning, purpose, and value, questions that lie beyond the purview of measurement, and deep within the heart of faith.

The two are not enemies. They are partners in truth.

In the end, the laws of thermodynamics whisper what faith proclaims with song:

- The universe is not arbitrary; it is governed by law.

- There is conservation at the heart of chaos.

- There is meaning in the decay.

- There is peace beyond the striving.

Science tells us how the world works. Faith tells us why it matters.

Together, they form a harmony not unlike a symphony, precise in structure, full of tension, yet moving always toward resolution.

And that resolution, faith says, is **not death, but renewal**. Not heat death, but rebirth. Not silence, but song.

III. The Law of Gravity Holding the Universe Together

Gravity is one of the four fundamental forces of nature. It is silent, invisible, and constant, binding galaxies, governing the tides, giving structure to the universe. Discovered formally by Sir Isaac Newton in the 17th century and later refined by Albert Einstein's general theory of relativity, gravity is far more than a physical law. It is also a metaphor for the unseen forces that draw us together: love, belonging, and the divine pull of faith.

Newton's equation, published in 1687, was revolutionary:

$$F=Gm1m2r2F = G \frac{m_1 m_2}{r^2}F=Gr2m1m2$$

Where:

- FFF is the gravitational force between two masses,

- GGG is the gravitational constant $(6.674\times10{-}11 \text{ Nm2/kg2} 6.674 \times 10^{-11} \,, \text{Nm}^2/\text{kg}^2 6.674\times10{-}11 \text{Nm2/kg2})$,

- $m1m\_1m1$ and $m2m\_2m2$ are the two masses,

- rrr is the distance between their centers.

This formula describes a universe held together by attraction, every mass, no matter how small, exerts a pull on every other mass.

This principle, universal and impartial, mirrors a spiritual truth: **everything matters**. There is no object or person too small to exert influence.

In 1915, Einstein published his general theory of relativity, replacing Newton's concept of gravity as a force with a new idea: **gravity is the warping of space-time caused by mass and energy**.

Imagine space-time as a rubber sheet. A massive object like the sun creates a dent in this sheet, and smaller objects (like planets) move along the curves created. They are not pulled; they are guided.

This elegant model aligns closely with how faith can guide the human spirit, not always through force, but through curvature and direction. God, like mass on space-time, shapes the terrain through which our lives move.

To the eye, gravity is invisible. But it is never absent. We don't see it, we feel it. We live by it. The same is true of faith.

In a gravitational field, the closer an object is to the source, the stronger the force. This is true in spiritual life as well: the closer the soul draws to the divine, the more deeply it feels the pull of love, grace, and meaning.

"Now faith is the assurance of things hoped for, the conviction of things not seen." —Hebrews 11:1

Gravity assures us that there is an unseen structure behind visible movement. Faith affirms the same: that behind what we experience, suffering, joy, longing, there is a deeper order.

In science, objects fall because they are obeying the curvature of space-time. They are not breaking the law; they are responding to it.

Spiritually, humans fall too, not because they are broken beyond redemption, but because they are moving through a broken world.

Just as terminal velocity defines the maximum speed an object reaches when falling through a medium (like air), there is a spiritual "velocity" in how we fall, limited, not limitless. We are not doomed to infinite descent.

Why?

Because gravity is not absolute, it is balanced by opposing forces. In the physical world, air resistance counters gravity. In the spiritual world, **grace** counters guilt, **hope** counters despair, and **love** pulls us back from the edge.

In science, weight is defined as:

$W = m \cdot g$

Where:

- **W** is weight,

- **m** is mass,

- **g** is the acceleration due to gravity (approximately $9.8 \, \text{m/s}^2$ on Earth).

Mass is constant; weight changes depending on the gravitational pull around it. And that simple law of physics holds a deeply spiritual truth.

Your **mass**, your value, your identity, doesn't change. It's steady, unshakable. But your **weight**, how you feel in the world, how burdened or light your soul feels, shifts with your surroundings.

When you're distant from God, life can feel unbearably heavy, like gravity has tightened its grip. But when you're walking in grace, when you're close to His presence, that same soul can feel light, almost weightless.

What surrounds you affects how you carry what's already within you.

C.S. Lewis captures this eloquently in *The Weight of Glory*:

"There are no ordinary people. You have never talked to a mere mortal."

He speaks not just of spiritual dignity but of a mass that cannot be reduced. Faith invites us to realize: **your existence has gravitational consequence**.

Black holes are regions of space where gravity is so intense that not even light can escape. At the center lies a singularity, an infinite density beyond current scientific understanding.

Spiritually, we encounter these "event horizons" too, moments of suffering, loss, or revelation, where everything familiar disappears and we face the unknowable.

Just as physicists approach black holes with both awe and caution, so the faithful approach the mystery of God, **not to solve, but to surrender**.

What keeps galaxies from tearing apart? Why doesn't the solar system collapse?

Because **forces are in balance**. Gravity draws. Inertia resists. The result: harmony.

Likewise, faith is not blind obedience. It is balance, between reason and wonder, order and surrender, reality and hope.

The gravitational constant GGG is unimaginably small. If it were slightly different, stars wouldn't form, life wouldn't exist. The universe is exquisitely fine-tuned.

This fine-tuning is not proof of God, but it is resonance, a cosmic harmony that faith hears as song:

"The heavens declare the glory of God; the skies proclaim the work of his hands." —Psalm 19:1

Gravity is always there, even when we don't notice. So is God.

The laws of nature are not separate from spiritual truth. They **whisper** it in numbers and formulas. They do not limit our faith, they deepen it.

We are held. Not by certainty, but by constancy. Not by sight, but by trust.

When we fall, we are not lost.

When we drift, we are not forgotten.

Because behind the motion of the cosmos and the longing of the soul, **there is something or Someone holding it all together**.

And that is the harmony of gravity and faith.

IV. The Laws of Motion

Sir Isaac Newton's three laws of motion, laid down in 1687, revolutionized how we understand physical reality. These principles describe how objects move, why they move, and what resists or initiates their movement. But beyond the realm of physics, these laws also hold a surprising resonance with the journey of the human spirit, how we grow, what moves us, and how our faith responds to resistance and force.

"An object at rest stays at rest, and an object in motion stays in motion unless acted upon by an external force."

This law speaks of **inertia**, the natural tendency of objects to resist change.

In life, we often find ourselves stuck in a state of spiritual inertia, stationary, complacent, or paralyzed by fear, guilt, or grief. We remain where we are because there is no force strong enough, or trusted enough, to move us.

Faith is that external force. It is the unseen hand that nudges us forward when we feel incapable of movement.

"With man this is impossible, but with God all things are possible." —Matthew 19:26

Just as a stationary object requires a push, so too do hearts caught in despair need the gentle but persistent force of love, truth, or grace. Faith is not simply belief, it is momentum.

"Force equals mass times acceleration."

$F = m \cdot a$

This law quantifies motion. It tells us that the force applied to an object determines its acceleration, depending on its mass.

In spiritual terms:

- **Mass** is the weight of our experience, our trauma, our past, our belief systems.

- **Acceleration** is our progress, emotional growth, healing, spiritual maturity.

- **Force** is faith, propelled by trust, prayer, purpose, and divine calling.

This law tells us that heavier souls, those carrying pain or burden, require more force to move. And yet, when that movement begins, it is a sacred shift.

Think of the woman in the Gospel who had bled for twelve years. When she touched the hem of Christ's garment, she was moved, not just physically, but spiritually. The force she exerted was not muscular, but faithful.

Faith generates acceleration, but it also respects mass. Some healing takes time. Some journeys are slower because the load is heavier.

"For every action, there is an equal and opposite reaction."

This law is about **balance**. Every push has a pushback. Every movement has consequence. Every act of love or harm sets something else in motion.

This principle reflects both justice and grace. In a mechanical universe, nothing happens in isolation. In the moral universe, the same is true.

When we forgive, it releases healing. When we act in anger, it fuels tension. When we pray, it is seen in unseen spaces.

"Whatever you sow, you will also reap." —Galatians 6:7

But here's where faith adds dimension. Grace is not bound by symmetry. It **disrupts the cycle**.

While science tells us that for every action there must be an equal and opposite reaction, faith tells us that mercy can break the equation. When we deserve judgment, we may receive forgiveness. When we sow in tears, we may reap in joy.

Science describes movement in terms of velocity, momentum, and mass. But motion is not always external. There is internal movement too, shifts in understanding, breakthroughs in healing, awakenings of conscience.

Faith honors both forms of movement.

There are seasons when we move outward, toward service, justice, connection. And there are seasons when we are called to be still, to rest, reflect, and listen.

"Be still, and know that I am God." —Psalm 46:10

Just as motion in physics is relative to the observer, spiritual movement is not always visible to others. You can look motionless and still be undergoing deep transformation. Like tectonic plates beneath the earth, some of the most powerful shifts are unseen.

In the real world, no object moves freely forever. It encounters **friction**, resistance from surfaces, air, or other forces.

So it is with our inner lives. Doubt, trauma, fear, criticism, self-sabotage, all are forms of friction. They oppose progress. They wear us down.

But friction, too, has purpose. Without it, we cannot stop. We cannot stabilize. Friction gives us traction, it slows us, teaches us, and allows moments of pause.

Faith does not promise a frictionless life. But it offers strength to overcome resistance, and a surface on which to stand.

When a soul is acted upon by the force of faith, it begins to move.

Sometimes that movement is swift and joyful, like a falling apple or a comet through the sky. Other times, it is labored and slow, like the turning of an old wheel. But in both cases, **something changes**.

Inertia is broken. Acceleration begins. The cycle of action and reaction is transformed by compassion.

And that is the harmony of motion and faith:

- Science teaches us **how** things move.

- Faith teaches us **why** they move and **where** they are going.

The universe is not static. Stars explode, planets orbit, galaxies collide. And within it, we move too, body and soul, pulled by forces visible and unseen.

Faith is not separate from this motion. It is embedded in it. It is what turns formula into meaning, and movement into purpose.

When Newton gave us his laws of motion, he revealed a God of order.

When we respond in faith, we experience a God of love.

And between the precision of physics and the poetry of the spirit, there is harmony, an elegant dance of law and grace, mass and mercy, force and forgiveness.

We are not aimless particles. We are pilgrims in motion, pulled by hope, propelled by faith, and sustained by the One who set the universe spinning in the first place.

The laws of nature are not divine, but they are divine in origin. They point not to a cold mechanism but to a wise Creator. They do not compete with the Gospel, they prepare us to receive it. For if the universe is so intricately ordered, how much more the Author of that order?

In the end, science gives us data. Faith gives us meaning. Together, they sing of a universe not just sustained by laws, but held by love.

Reflective Questions

Imagine God writing the laws of physics not just to govern the universe, but to teach us something about faithfulness, balance, and timing. What lesson might He be teaching you right now?

_____

_____

_____

_____

If nature obeys without question, trees growing toward light, rivers flowing to the sea, what would it look like for your heart to align with that same quiet obedience?

_____

_____

_____

_____

When you observe the precision of planetary motion or the rhythm of the tides, do you feel a longing to live with that same sense of divine rhythm? What keeps you in sync, or out of sync, with it?

_____

_____

_____

If gravity never forgets to hold you to the Earth, what does that say about a God who never forgets to hold your soul?

Chapter 5
The Genesis of Life

'Taste and see that the Lord is good...' (Psalm 34:8)

I. The Marvel of Biochemistry

Life does not begin in grand gestures, but in the quiet. In a space too small for the eye to see, something astonishing happens. Inside every living cell, a kind of miracle unfolds every second. Molecules find each other in the dark. Proteins twist into perfect shapes. Tiny engines spin to make energy. Instructions stored in DNA are read, copied, and carried out with precision. There is no chaos here, only order, balance, and breathtaking detail.

Science calls it biochemistry.

Some call it design.

Is it all the result of chance, billions of random changes over time? Or does the elegance suggest intention? For many, the cell is not just a machine. It's a message. A clue. A whisper that we are not accidents. That we were made.

From the simplest prokaryote to the most intricate eukaryotic cell, life is an architecture of breathtaking ingenuity. The eukaryotic cell, in particular, is a self-contained metropolis, a walled city of purpose. Each component, from the nucleus that safeguards the genetic script to the mitochondria that burn fuel into usable energy, contributes to a balanced whole. The endoplasmic reticulum folds proteins like origami. The Golgi apparatus dispatches them with postal precision. Lysosomes recycle the old to make way for the new.

And in the heart of this city spins ATP synthase, a molecular motor embedded in mitochondrial membranes. It rotates with elegant efficiency, turning proton gradients into packets of energy called ATP, the currency of cellular life. Each revolution crafts life's momentum. At the nanoscale, it is as intricate as any machine conceived by human hands, and orders of magnitude smaller.

Then there are the enzymes, the quiet artisans of biochemistry. Each one is a marvel of specificity, fitting its substrate like a lock and key, catalyzing reactions with unimaginable speed. Carbonic anhydrase, for example, can facilitate up to a million reactions per second, balancing blood pH with grace and speed. These molecular agents know what to do, when to act, and how to correct themselves if they falter.

All of this is choreographed through homeostasis, the body's internal harmony. Through countless biochemical feedback loops, the cell maintains temperature, pH, nutrient levels, and electrical charge. It is a system that listens, responds, and adapts, like a living prayer of equilibrium.

And yet, even these intricate systems hint at something more provocative. Michael Behe, in his theory of irreducible complexity, posits that certain biological structures, like the bacterial flagellum, a whip-like rotor used for movement, require all their parts to function. Remove one, and the whole collapses. These systems do not seem to lend themselves to slow, stepwise evolution. They work only when whole, complete, and integrated. How then, one might ask, could such structures arise by chance?

Though controversial in academic circles, the question lingers. The mechanisms of natural selection are elegant, but are they sufficient? Can blind forces sculpt complexity so refined? Or does the irreducible nature of these systems point to a mind behind matter, a composer behind the code?

The very blueprints of life, the Krebs Cycle, DNA replication, protein synthesis, are built from chains of reactions so interdependent that they evoke the ancient philosophical dilemma: which came first, the chicken or the egg?

The Krebs Cycle, for instance, is not merely a loop of reactions that generate cellular fuel. It is a web of precision where each molecule hands off its electrons in perfect timing. DNA, the vault of genetic memory, must be faithfully copied, but the enzymes that perform this feat are themselves encoded within DNA. How then did the system bootstrap itself into being?

Each pathway depends on another; each part is both result and prerequisite. This recursive complexity raises a profound and humbling question: is such a system even plausible without a guiding intelligence?

"I praise you," the Psalmist wrote, "because I am fearfully and wonderfully made."

Indeed, in the complex design of biochemistry, awe finds its home. This is not a randomness scattered in molecular dust, but a choreography that invites reverence. Whether one sees it as divine architecture or the poetry of atoms, it is hard not to be moved by the majesty it unveils.

Here, at the edge of biology and mystery, we find a meeting place, where science uncovers *how*, and faith whispers *why*.

II. The Language of DNA

Before we take our first breath, before our hearts begin to beat or our limbs begin to form, a message is already being read. Not from a book. Not from a voice. But from a code, whispered deep within the nucleus of every cell.

This code is DNA, a molecule so rich with meaning, so precise in function, and so elegant in design that scientists call it the blueprint of life. But blueprints are drawn by architects. Scripts are written by authors. And to many, DNA feels like more than mere molecules. It feels like a message, intended, not accidental.

DNA is made up of just four simple chemical bases: adenine (A), thymine (T), cytosine (C), and guanine (G). But these are not just molecules. They are letters in a divine alphabet, carefully chosen, precisely arranged. A pairs with T, and C with G, forming the elegant, spiraling staircase of the double helix.

But what gives DNA its power is not just the structure, it's the sequence. The sacred order of these letters whispers instructions into every cell: how to form muscles that move, nerves that feel, skin that protects, blood that gives life, memory that stores our story, and emotions that stir our soul.

Within the more than 3 billion base pairs of the human genome lies the blueprint for over 20,000 proteins, each one a small miracle. Together, they orchestrate everything from the rhythm of our heartbeat to the color of our eyes.

This is not random. This is not chaos. This is intentional. You were written into existence: letter by letter, strand by strand by a Creator who speaks in the language of life.

According to Claude Shannon's Information Theory, information is not just noise, it is a measurable, encoded message. DNA, with its redundancy, error correction, and data compression features, mirrors the structure of man-made codes. It behaves like software. It carries syntax, grammar, instruction. And yet it predates all human language.

So we are faced with a question:

Can chance arrange this much meaning out of molecules?

Can a random process write a working sentence, let alone the encyclopedia written into every one of our cells?

You see, DNA doesn't just store information, it knows when to speak.

Every cell in your body contains the same DNA, yet some become skin while others become bone or brain. This is because of gene expression, a process that controls which parts of the DNA are read, and when.

Think of it as a musical score. The notes are all written down, but the conductor decides which section plays, when to crescendo, when to pause.

Proteins known as transcription factors act like master conductors of life's orchestra. They don't make a sound themselves, yet with perfect timing, they cue the instruments, activating or silencing genes exactly when needed. One note too early, one beat too late, and the whole symphony of the body falters.

And beyond even this intricate dance lies **epigenetics**, a mysterious, tender layer of control that responds not just to biology, but to **life itself**. Our experiences, our environments, even our **emotions**, can open or close the pages of our genetic script. Like a divine dimmer switch, epigenetics can quiet one gene and awaken another, bringing nuance and depth to the story written in our DNA.

But perhaps the most breathtaking of all are the **HOX genes**, a handful of master switches that determine the entire architecture of the human body. These genes speak with unimaginable authority, telling cells: "Here, the head. There, the spine. Now, shape the arms, the hands, the heart." They choreograph creation with staggering precision. And if just one HOX gene strays from its role, the blueprint changes, the very form of the body reshaped.

This is not coincidence. It is **holy orchestration**. A testament that from the moment of conception, your body has been guided by invisible hands, through music, memory, and miracles.

It is a system too complex to be careless. Too precise to be random. Too eloquent not to be called language.

And yet, even this code would be useless without the machinery to read it, copy it, and protect it.

The enzyme DNA polymerase acts like a molecular scribe. As it copies DNA during cell division, it scans each base and corrects mistakes with astonishing efficiency, making only about one error in every 10 billion bases. It edits as it writes.

Then there is the ribosome, often called the most sophisticated machine in nature. This tiny molecular factory reads messenger RNA, transcribed from DNA, and assembles amino acids into proteins, one by one, like beads on a string. It does this with accuracy, speed, and purpose, billions of times each day in each human body.

These machines don't just function, they exhibit intelligence-like behavior. They follow logic. They detect and fix errors. They respond to their environment. No machine humans have ever made rivals their efficiency, and yet they emerged, some say, without intention?

To call this *natural selection* without acknowledging the brilliance of the system is like calling the Mona Lisa a water stain.

"In the beginning was the Word..." (John 1:1)

It is no accident that the Bible begins with language. Not fire. Not steel. Not force. But a Word.

God *spoke*, and light came. He *said*, and stars obeyed. His breath became biology. His voice became code.

And what is DNA, if not a kind of word? A message written in four letters. A sacred script repeated through every living thing. Genesis tells us that "God said..." and it was so. And now, every time a cell divides, every time life continues, the cell repeats what it was first told.

Science has decoded the letters. But the Author? That mystery still hums through the nucleus like a heartbeat.

III. The Anthropic Principle and Fine-Tuning

Before the first cell pulsed with life, before stars kindled in the vacuum of space, something was already astonishingly, impossibly precise. It is as though the dials of the universe had been tuned, each one aligned to an exact frequency that permits life to exist at all. This is the essence of the Anthropic Principle: that the universe appears not indifferent, but *tailored*, as if expecting us.

This idea does not rest in abstraction or philosophy alone. It finds its footing in chemistry, physics, and mathematics, where the numbers speak, and what they say is breathtaking.

Life, as we know it, hangs in a delicate balance. If even a single variable shifted slightly, the system would collapse, not gradually, but instantly.

• pH Ranges and Enzymes

Enzymes, the molecular machines that sustain metabolism, are exquisitely sensitive. Most function only within narrow pH ranges, typically between 6.5 and 7.5. Just a small shift in acidity or alkalinity can denature them, unraveling their shape and silencing their function.

Why should such delicate parameters exist at all? And why does Earth just happen to provide the perfect range?

110

• Water: The Silent Miracle

Water, so common we forget its strangeness, is an anomaly in the universe. Its polarity allows it to dissolve countless substances, making it the universal solvent essential to life. Its high specific heat regulates climate and internal body temperatures. Its solid form floats, insulating lakes and oceans from freezing solid.

Every property of water: surface tension, cohesion, boiling point, seems to have been finely set, as if written into the script of life.

• Temperature Sensitivity in Proteins

Proteins, constructed from chains of amino acids, fold into intricate three-dimensional shapes. These folds determine their function, and even a slight increase in temperature can cause these structures to collapse. Life depends on an extraordinarily narrow thermal window.

Why does Earth orbit a star at just the right distance to keep temperatures in this precious range?

• Hydrogen Bonding and DNA Stability

The double helix of DNA is held together by hydrogen bonds, strong enough to maintain structure, weak enough to allow unzipping for replication. Alter the strength of these bonds even slightly, and DNA either disintegrates or locks shut, unreadable.

This is not randomness. This is symmetry. Precision. It is as though life walks a tightrope, and the rope stretches across the laws of the cosmos.

Imagine trying to form a single functional protein, the kind required for even the simplest life. Let's say it's 150 amino acids long. Since there are 20 standard amino acids, the total number of possible combinations is:

$$20^{150} = 10^{195}$$

That's a 1 followed by 195 zeroes.

For comparison, the number of atoms in the entire observable universe is estimated at only 10^{80}.

And that's for *one* protein. Life needs thousands, all interacting in specific, timely sequences.

Even granting billions of years and trillions of chemical reactions, the odds remain so astronomically small that many scientists compare them to the chance of a tornado assembling a functioning jet out of scrap metal.

Is this merely coincidence?

Even Nobel Prize-winning physicist Roger Penrose calculated that the odds of the universe's initial conditions being suitable for life by chance alone is 1 in $10^{10^{123}}$, a number so large it defies imagination. He called it *"extraordinary beyond reason."*

"For since the creation of the world God's invisible qualities, his eternal power and divine nature, have been clearly seen, being understood from what has been made..." *(Romans 1:20)*

We do not see the hand that tuned the dials, but we live in the warmth of its touch.

Fine-tuning does not *prove* God. But it invites us to wonder. It opens the door to the possibility that we were not accidental products of chaos, but the intended recipients of care. A care written into the code, measured in molecules, and whispered through water, heat, and light.

What if the precision of hydrogen bonds, the fragility of enzyme function, and the symmetry of DNA are not flukes, but signatures? What if life isn't just *possible*, but *wanted*?

IV. Current Scientific and Religious Dialogue

In the modern world, it is often claimed that faith and science live in tension, two languages spoken by opposing tribes. But this is a false dichotomy. The human mind, after all, was crafted to ask both *how* and *why*, to explore the mechanisms of the cosmos and also its meaning. Beneath the surface of apparent conflict lies something far more profound: a dialogue that is still evolving, still alive, and still shaping the way we see the universe, and ourselves.

The idea of Darwinian evolution, life evolving through random mutation and natural selection, has become a foundational principle of modern biology. From bacteria to butterflies to human beings, Darwin's theory offers a coherent, testable framework to explain biodiversity. Yet, as our tools sharpen and our microscopes magnify, some begin to ask: is this explanation sufficient? Can chance and necessity alone account for the breathtaking intricacy of life?

Enter the theory of Intelligent Design (ID).

• Intelligent Design

Intelligent Design does not reject evolution outright. Instead, it challenges the assumption that all complexity can be explained through blind processes. ID theorists, biochemists, philosophers, and physicists among them, argue that certain features of biological systems exhibit hallmarks of purposeful engineering:

- The rotating engine of the bacterial flagellum.
- The layered editing and repair systems of DNA.

- The digital-like coding of the genetic alphabet.

- The irreducible interdependence of biochemical pathways.

ID stops short of naming the designer; it is not theology but an inference grounded in empirical observation. Critics protest that it lacks predictive power or falsifiability, but defenders argue that design is a valid scientific hypothesis, just as the search for extraterrestrial intelligence relies on recognizing patterns that are too precise to be random.

They ask: *If we would infer design upon discovering a radio signal from space composed of prime numbers, why not infer it when we see highly specified, information-rich DNA sequences building life?*

The real tension, then, is not between science and faith, but between worldviews: one that sees only natural law, and one that suspects a lawgiver.

There are many who walk between these poles, who refuse to choose between evolution and belief. This is the path of Theistic Evolution, or what some call Evolutionary Creationism.

This view, championed by theologians and scientists alike, asserts that God used evolution as His creative instrument, that the processes we observe are not godless, but guided by divine wisdom. The randomness of mutations, they say, does not imply chaos, but the unfolding of possibility within boundaries set by the Creator.

Organizations like the BioLogos Foundation, founded by renowned geneticist Francis Collins, argue passionately for this reconciliation. To them:

- The book of nature and the book of Scripture both speak truth.

114

- Evolution explains the *mechanism*, but God remains the author.

- Science and faith, when rightly understood, do not contradict but complete one another.

Theistic evolution holds a reverence for Scripture without clinging to literalism that may conflict with evidence. Genesis is seen not as a lab report, but as a cosmic hymn, a sacred declaration that God made the heavens and the earth, and called them good.

This view appeals to many Christians who accept the robust data behind evolution but refuse to see life as accidental. For them, God is still the Prime Mover, the Composer of the grand biological symphony.

It is often said, falsely, that the more scientific you become, the less room you have for God. Yet the evidence tells another story.

Dr. Francis Collins, who led the international effort to sequence the human genome, once knelt in awe on a mountaintop and gave his life to Christ. For Collins, reading the 3.1 billion letters of DNA was like reading the language of God, the software of life, coded in adenine, thymine, cytosine, and guanine.

He is not alone.

According to a 2009 Pew Research Center survey, approximately 60% of American scientists profess belief in a higher power or spiritual force. Among Nobel Laureates, many have been outspoken in their belief that science does not erase mystery, it amplifies it.

Werner Heisenberg, father of quantum mechanics, said: *"The first gulp from the glass of natural sciences will turn you into an atheist, but at the bottom of the glass God is waiting."*

Arthur Compton, winner of the Nobel Prize in Physics, believed: *"The chance of life originating from accident is comparable to the chance of the complete Oxford dictionary resulting from an explosion in a print shop."*

Max Planck, the founder of quantum theory, once stated: *"Both religion and science require a belief in God. For believers, God is in the beginning, and for physicists, He is at the end of all considerations."*

These were not men who retreated from science to find God. They found God in the very structure of the universe.

We stand at a powerful crossroad in history. Never before has humanity known so much about its biology, its cosmos, and its origins. And yet, never before have we needed more wisdom to interpret that knowledge.

In this ongoing dialogue between science and faith, some see contradiction. Others see harmony. The same laws that govern stars also shape DNA. The same brain that maps galaxies also yearns for meaning.

It is not unreasonable to believe that truth may come from both microscope and manuscript, from quantum field and sacred text. If there is a Creator, then surely He is not threatened by our discoveries, but rather, revealed by them.

Science may teach us how the symphony plays. But perhaps faith tells us who wrote the music.

V. Practical Implications

As we explore the breathtaking intricacy of biochemistry and DNA, we are not merely studying atoms and enzymes, we are standing before a mirror reflecting profound ethical, philosophical, and spiritual questions. If life bears the hallmarks of a Creator's signature, then how we treat that life carries immense moral weight.

When we consider that life may be not only functional but intentionally designed, the ethical stakes of our actions escalate profoundly. If DNA is not a meaningless chemical accident, but rather a sacred script authored with intelligence, then the laboratory becomes a kind of modern-day temple, where human hands must tread with reverence, not recklessness.

The power to alter the human genome now rests in our grasp. With tools like CRISPR-Cas9, we can splice, insert, or silence genes with increasing precision. While this offers hope for treating inherited diseases like cystic fibrosis, Huntington's disease, and sickle cell anemia, it also tempts us to move beyond healing into enhancement.

- Should we engineer children to be taller, stronger, or more intelligent?

- What happens to the value of an unmodified life when we begin to "customize" the next generation?

- Do we risk creating genetic underclasses, those who can afford such edits, and those who cannot?

If life is sacred, designed rather than accidental, then it cannot be upgraded like software. The idea of editing human potential raises ancient moral questions in a modern form: Who gets to decide what is "better"? Who plays God?

The birth of Dolly the sheep in 1996 marked the dawn of a new era in biotechnology: cloning was no longer science fiction. Since then, the concept of cloning humans has hovered uncomfortably on the ethical horizon. If we clone a person, do we clone their soul, their identity, their destiny? Would a clone have the same dignity, the same spiritual essence? Is replicating human life an act of healing or hubris?

In a worldview that sees each person as fearfully and wonderfully made, the act of replication cannot be morally neutral. Cloning challenges our ideas of uniqueness, personhood, and divine intention.

Scientists today can design and construct entirely new life forms using synthetic biology. In 2010, researchers at the J. Craig Venter Institute created the first synthetic bacterial cell, powered by a genome assembled from scratch.

This raises profound questions. If we create life, are we creating something sacred or something soulless? Does synthetic life have moral status? Where is the line between creation and fabrication?

If life originates from a Creator, then mimicking the creative process carries not only power but moral peril. We may be advancing technically, but are we evolving ethically?

Embryonic stem cells hold incredible promise for regenerating tissues and treating diseases such as Parkinson's and diabetes. But obtaining these cells often involves destroying human embryos. At what point does life begin? Is an embryo merely a clump of cells or a being infused with purpose? If we believe life is designed from the moment of conception, do we not owe it protection?

Alternatives like induced pluripotent stem cells (iPSCs) are helping bridge the divide between progress and principle, but the debate still burns at the heart of science and faith.

Also, with advanced medicine prolonging life, decisions about how and when to die have grown more complex. In some countries, physician-assisted suicide is legal, raising ethical questions:

- Is suffering always something to be avoided?

- Does the right to die diminish the value of life?

- Can ending a life ever be an act of reverence, or is it a denial of life's sacredness?

If we see every breath as intentional and imbued with divine design, we must carefully weigh compassion against conviction.

In all these developments, a central question emerges: Are we caretakers or creators?

The biblical concept of stewardship (Genesis 2:15) calls humanity to tend and protect creation, not to dominate or distort it. Bioethics rooted in this view recognizes the beauty of science, its potential to heal, restore, and enlighten, but insists that science must be governed by conscience. It is not anti-science to ask hard questions. It is not anti-progress to pause before profound change. It is not weakness to act with humility. In a world increasingly capable of shaping life itself, our restraint may prove more godlike than our power.

In the quiet hum of a laboratory, surrounded by equations and genetic sequences, many scientists encounter not sterility, but sacredness. The deeper they descend into the machinery of life, the louder the whisper of mystery becomes.

To observe how DNA polymerase proofreads a genome or how ATP synthase spins like a microscopic turbine is to witness a silent miracle. These are not just chemical processes; they are acts of astonishing precision, unfolding billions of times within us every second.

For many, this awe becomes a form of worship.

- Albert Einstein, who marveled at the laws of physics, declared: *"Science without religion is lame, religion without science is blind."*

- Carl Sagan, an agnostic, wrote of the cosmos with sacred reverence: *"For small creatures such as we, the vastness is bearable only through love."*

- Countless researchers, including Francis Collins, speak of moments in science that feel like encounters with the divine, not because they *cannot* be explained, but because they are so beautifully ordered.

Scientific discovery, at its highest, is not a rejection of faith. It is an invitation into deeper reverence, a call to recognize the logic behind the leaf, the architecture in the atom, and the intelligence in the invisible.

When a person stands before the double helix, they may not hear a voice from heaven. But they might still sense that the code before them was written, not merely formed.

Biochemistry and DNA are not chaotic. They are not clumsy, not accidental, not patched together by random forces fumbling in the dark. Instead, they reveal a world elegantly tuned, finely structured, and astonishingly self-sustaining.

- The cell, in all its microscopic splendor, behaves like a city.

- The genome reads like a language.

- The ribosome assembles like a craftsman.

- The enzymes operate like engineers.

Each molecule whispers that life is not a fluke, it is engineered with wisdom, sustained with precision, and coded with intent.

Where some see only chemistry, others glimpse the face of a Designer. Where some speak of survival, others hear the sound of sacredness.

Reflective Questions

If enzymes speed up the reactions that sustain life, what are the "spiritual enzymes" in your life, those unseen graces that help you grow, heal, and move forward?

_____

_____

_____

_____

DNA carries your blueprint, but who whispered the first instruction? What does it mean to you that every cell echoes a sacred design?

_____

_____

_____

_____

Biochemistry shows us that even the tiniest imbalance can affect the whole body. What spiritual imbalances have you been ignoring, and what might restoration look like at the soul level?

_____

_____

_____

_____

Chapter 6
The Complexity of Cosmos

What do you see when you look up at the sky?

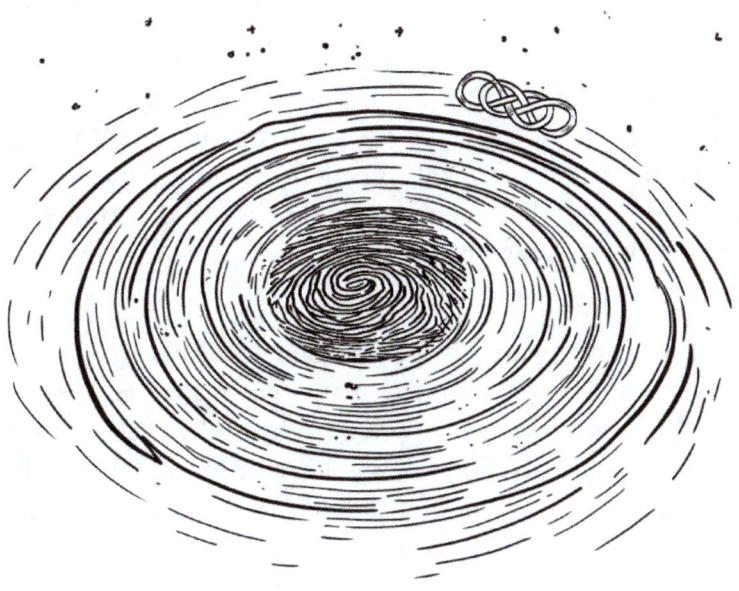

'The heavens declare the glory of God...' – Psalm 19:1

There is something timeless about looking up at the night sky. For a moment, all the noise of life falls away, the deadlines, the decisions, the dull ache of daily repetition. In its place comes a stillness that feels almost ancient. The stars, scattered like diamonds across a canvas of endless black, do not shout or dazzle. They whisper. And in that whisper is a question as old as humanity itself.

We have always looked up. Long before telescopes, before science had names for constellations or formulas for gravity, people lifted their eyes to the heavens and felt something stir. Awe. Longing. Reverence. The stars were more than lights; they were signs. Guides for sailors, muses for poets, symbols for prophets. They mapped not only the skies, but the soul's deep need for meaning.

It is no coincidence that the oldest stories ever told are written in the language of the stars. We named them after gods and heroes, built temples in alignment with their patterns, and measured time by their rising and setting. Somehow, instinctively, we knew that the cosmos was not random. It was speaking. It was alive with intention.

And now, even with all our knowledge, all our theories of expansion and entropy, of dark matter and distant galaxies, we are still left with the same wonder: Why? Why such vastness, such impossible precision? Why a universe so finely tuned that the difference between life and lifelessness balances on a razor's edge?

Is this grand structure, this breathtaking architecture of light and distance and law, a cosmic accident? Or is it a canvas, carefully stretched, skillfully painted by a divine hand that not only sees the whole but also cherishes the smallest spark?

To stare at the night sky is to remember: we are not adrift. We are part of something vast, deliberate, and deeply beautiful. Something that humbles us, and at the same time, makes us feel profoundly seen.

I. A Universe Measured to Breathe Life

It is one of the most staggering truths of our existence: the universe, in all its grandeur and complexity, appears to be exquisitely, almost impossibly, fine-tuned for life.

At the foundation of everything, beyond atoms and elements, beyond light and time, are a set of physical constants. They are the invisible rules by which everything operates, the silent agreements written into the structure of reality itself. These constants do not drift or vary. They do not adjust based on location or mood. They are unchanging, unwavering, and unimaginably precise.

Take the **gravitational constant**, for example, the force that holds galaxies together, keeps planets in orbit, and pins our feet gently to the ground. If gravity were just slightly weaker, stars could not form; if slightly stronger, they would burn too hot and too fast for life to ever begin. Even a minuscule change, by as little as one part in 10^{60}, would render the cosmos sterile.

Or consider the **speed of light**, a speed that governs how energy moves, how time bends, how causality works. It is not just a number; it is a boundary, a heartbeat of the universe. If it were slightly different, the balance of mass and energy would collapse. Stars might never ignite. Chemistry as we know it would not exist.

The **electromagnetic force** is what holds electrons in orbit around nuclei, allowing atoms to form molecules, and molecules to become the building blocks of life. If it were slightly stronger or weaker, atoms could not bond in the ways needed to sustain complex chemistry. Life's language would never be spoken.

Then there are the **strong and weak nuclear forces**, the powers that hold the heart of atoms together and govern radioactive decay. Their precise balance allows stars to burn steadily, forging the heavier elements like carbon and oxygen that make up our bodies. Alter one of these forces by even the tiniest fraction, and the stars themselves could not sustain the fire of life.

It is as if the universe is built on a control panel, a massive console with dozens of dials. Each dial represents one of these fundamental constants. But here's the astonishing part: each dial is tuned not roughly, not approximately, but *exactly*. If even one of these dials were turned slightly left or right, even by a hair's width, the universe would not permit life, not just human life, but any form of organized, stable complexity. No planets. No cells. No breath. No being.

The odds of all of these dials aligning precisely are so small that they stagger even the most skeptical minds. This is not just complexity. It is intentionality written into the laws of existence. It is as though Someone knew we were coming.

Some argue that it's coincidence. That we simply find ourselves in a rare and lucky universe where everything happened to fall into place. But others, those who dare to believe in design, see something more. They see a signature. A whisper of care and foresight, not just in biology, not just in beauty, but in the very numbers that hold the cosmos together.

How could such improbable precision arise from chaos alone? Can we truly attribute this breathtaking balance to chance?

Or dare we consider that behind the equations and forces and figures, there is a Mind. A Designer. A God who not only created the stars but also tuned them to burn with the exact warmth to make us wonder, to give us breath, to lead us to ask, "What does it mean that the universe wanted me here?"

The fine-tuning of the universe is not just a scientific observation, it is a spiritual invitation. To look beyond what is, and ask who set the dials. To look at the sky and know: this was not an accident. It was a gift.

II. The Beauty and Order in the Heavens

We live on a fragile sphere, suspended in a void so vast we can scarcely fathom its edges. And yet, within that unfathomable expanse, our planet spins calmly, perfectly poised in a place where life not only exists, but flourishes. It is easy to take this for granted. But when we pause, when we look closer, we begin to see the fingerprints of something greater, etched not just in the biology of our bodies, but in the physics of the heavens.

One of the most poetic truths of our existence is this: Earth resides in what astronomers call the "Goldilocks Zone." Not too close to the sun, not too far away…just right. Were we even a little closer, the oceans would boil, and our atmosphere would collapse under a runaway greenhouse effect. A little farther, and water would freeze, turning Earth into a lifeless ball of ice. But we are not too close. We are not too far. We are exactly where we need to be. Just right.

This placement is not merely convenient, it is essential. The Goldilocks Zone allows water to exist in all three states: liquid, solid, and gas. It permits complex weather systems, the regulation of climate, and the intricate chemical reactions necessary for life. And while we marvel at the beauty of sunsets and the rhythm of seasons, we often forget: those wonders are only possible because Earth orbits at just the right distance, at just the right speed, with just the right tilt.

But Earth's hospitality does not end there. In the celestial theater, we are not alone in our protection. Jupiter, massive and mighty, plays the role of cosmic guardian. Its enormous gravitational pull acts as a shield, deflecting countless asteroids and comets that might otherwise bombard our fragile world. Without Jupiter standing in the outer reaches, sweeping the solar system with its vast invisible arms, life on Earth might have never had the chance to begin.

Then there is our Moon, a companion whose quiet presence shapes the rhythm of life. Its gravitational tug gives rise to the tides, nurturing marine ecosystems, influencing weather, and perhaps even stabilizing Earth's axial tilt. That tilt, in turn, governs our seasons, creating the balance of heat and cold that allows ecosystems to flourish. Without the Moon's stabilizing pull, Earth might wobble like a spinning top, swinging chaotically between climate extremes.

And beneath our feet, another miracle: Earth's magnetic field. Generated by the churning of molten iron in our planet's core, this invisible barrier wraps around us like a shield. It deflects deadly solar winds and cosmic radiation, without which our atmosphere would be stripped away, and life, if it could begin at all, would struggle to endure. That such a field exists, and persists, is yet another thread in the web of conditions that make this planet not just habitable, but hospitable.

When you step back and look at the whole, Earth in the habitable zone, protected by Jupiter, stabilized by the Moon, shielded by a magnetic field, you begin to sense something deeper. Something almost...intentional. Could this delicate arrangement be the product of chance? Or does it bear the signature of a cosmic Artist, who not only created a universe, but prepared a home within it?

The mechanics of the heavens only deepen the wonder. Planets move with breathtaking precision, dancing around the sun in ellipses described centuries ago by Kepler. Their paths are governed by laws so elegant, so consistent, that we can predict eclipses, tides, and planetary alignments with astonishing accuracy. Newton's laws of motion, Einstein's curvature of space-time, the orbital resonances and gravitational harmonies, they do not speak of chaos. They speak of order. Of a mind behind the motion. Of purpose wrapped in poetry.

And in all of this, we hear an ancient echo:

"The heavens declare the glory of God; the skies proclaim the work of His hands." — *Psalm 19:1*

This verse, written long before telescopes or satellites, captures what the soul has always known. That the cosmos, in all its vastness and intricacy, is not silent. It declares. It proclaims. Not only with beauty, but with balance. Not only with distance, but with detail.

And what does it declare? Not merely power or intelligence, but glory. A glory that speaks to something beyond utility. A glory that says we are not here by accident. That perhaps, the same God who numbered the stars also thought the Earth worth preparing. That maybe, just maybe, our place in the cosmos is not an oversight, but a gift.

And yet, here lies the paradox. When we look up at the stars, at galaxies billions of light-years away, at nebulae birthing suns, we feel our smallness. We are tiny, fragile, dust-bound beings. One planet among billions. One life among many. And still, we feel something else too. We feel significance. Not in spite of our smallness, but *because* of it. As though the vastness of the universe exists not to diminish us, but to awaken awe. As though we are meant to see the scale and ask, "What kind of love sets all this in motion, and still sees me?"

This is the emotional truth of the cosmos. It humbles and uplifts. It silences and sings. It reminds us that the One who made the stars may have also made a place for us, not just to survive, but to wonder, to love, to ask deep questions of purpose and belonging.

To live on Earth is to be invited into a miracle. Not just a scientific marvel, but a spiritual one. A story written not only in particles and photons, but in meaning and mercy.

So the next time you look at the Moon rising, or feel the tides draw back, or watch a sunrise gild the edges of morning, remember: you are part of a cosmic choreography more beautiful and intentional than words can fully capture. And it all begins with a planet placed *just right*, in a universe that whispers: **you were meant to be here.**

III. Of Stars and Souls: The Universe That Knew We Were Coming

There is a quiet whisper in the cosmos, one that grows louder the more we learn. It is not found in religious texts or philosophical treatises alone, but in physics equations, starlight, and the periodic table. It speaks of a universe not only capable of sustaining life but seemingly *tailored* for it. This is the heart of the anthropic principle, the idea that the universe appears, in its laws and constants, to be precisely calibrated for the existence of life, and more specifically, for human beings.

From the strength of gravity to the ratio of the electromagnetic force, from the speed of light to the masses of subatomic particles, every thread in the fabric of reality appears exquisitely tuned. A little stronger here, a little weaker there, and atoms couldn't form. Stars wouldn't ignite. Molecules wouldn't bind.

Life would never have stood a chance. And yet, here we are. Not just existing, but aware. Reflecting. Asking. Wondering why.

Some call this divine design. Others call it coincidence. In an attempt to explain this improbable harmony without invoking intentionality, the multiverse theory has emerged from the world of theoretical physics. It proposes that our universe is just one among countless others, each with its own set of physical laws and constants. In most of these hypothetical universes, life is impossible. But in ours, by sheer chance, the dials happened to align just right. And so, we are here, simply because we *could* be.

This explanation is both awe-inspiring and sobering. The multiverse doesn't deny wonder, it multiplies it. But does it answer the deeper longing of the human heart? Or does it, in trying to remove purpose, miss the poetry?

Some argue that if there are infinite universes, ours is not special. That our existence is not designed, but inevitable somewhere. But perhaps this misses the deeper truth. For even if there are a million universes, or a billion, it does not dilute the beauty of ours. It expands the canvas of divine creativity. What kind of God, after all, would be limited to *one* universe? Why wouldn't a Creator who delights in variation and abundance sow stars across every possibility, crafting life in ways we've yet to imagine?

Far from erasing purpose, the idea of a multiverse could point to an even grander vision, a divine mind so expansive, so boundless, that it plays in infinity and still chooses to be intimately present in *this* one. In *your* life. In *our* story.

And it is a beautiful story.

Long before we drew breath, the elements of our bodies were forged in the hearts of dying stars. Carbon, calcium, iron, the building blocks of life, were born not on Earth, but in the nuclear furnaces of ancient suns. When massive stars exhausted their fuel, they collapsed in on themselves and exploded in brilliant supernovae, scattering their elemental riches across the cosmos. These atoms drifted through the void, gathered into clouds, condensed into planets, and one day, into *us*.

Carl Sagan said it with poetic clarity: **"We are made of star stuff."** And it's more than science, it is sacred. It means that the very substance of our being has a history written in fire and light. That the Creator, rather than forming us from sterile matter, chose instead the dust of stars as our raw material. That before we ever cried, or spoke, or loved, we were already part of the heavens.

There is something profoundly humbling in that. To think that every heartbeat is powered by atoms with a cosmic ancestry. That when we lift our eyes to the night sky, we are not looking at something "out there" we are looking at where we came from. The universe is not merely our backdrop; it is our birthplace. And perhaps that's why it stirs us so deeply. Why silence falls when we stare at stars. Why tears come unbidden under a canopy of galaxies. Some ancient part of us remembers.

But this story doesn't end in stardust. For while the elements of our bodies came from stars, the spark that animates us, the consciousness, the soul, the capacity to love and to choose, speaks of something beyond physics. No amount of gravity or fusion explains the ache for meaning. No chemical reaction accounts for the longing for eternity. We are not just biological. We are spiritual. Not just formed, we are *intended*.

And if that is true, then every proton and photon, every constant and quark, every cosmic law and celestial rhythm, has been part of a divine symphony, one that culminates not in galaxies or black holes, but in the human heart. In the capacity for worship. In the sacred hunger to know our Maker.

Some may ask: Isn't that arrogant? To think the universe exists for us? But it is not arrogance it is astonishment. For we are small, yes, heartbreakingly so. Our lives are brief flickers in a cosmos billions of years old. And yet, in our smallness, we are seen. In our brevity, we are loved. In our fragility, we are chosen.

This is the paradox of faith and science: The more we understand the universe, the more improbable our existence becomes, and the more sacred it begins to feel. Science reveals how finely tuned everything is; faith whispers why. Science describes the mechanism; faith contemplates the meaning. Together, they do not contradict, they harmonize.

And perhaps this is the ultimate message of the anthropic principle. Not merely that the universe allows for life, but that it *anticipated* life. That the cosmos, in its 13.8 billion-year journey, has been preparing a place for beings who could love, wonder, hope, and worship. And if the universe knew we were coming, perhaps it's because the One who made it wrote us into the script from the beginning.

So tonight, if you find yourself under a starry sky, take a breath. Feel the ground beneath you, formed from ancient ash. Look up. And remember: You are part of a story far older and deeper than you imagined. One written in atoms and light, in purpose and fire. A story in which the Author is both the Maker of stars, and the Lover of souls.

IV. Awe as a Path to Worship

There is a silence that only the stars can teach. It descends on us when we stand under a dark sky, far from the noise of city lights, and lift our eyes upward. Something ancient stirs, older than language, deeper than thought. A sense that we are part of something vast, something intricate and beautiful, something that refuses to be tamed by explanation alone. This silence is not empty. It is full of awe. And awe, when allowed to run its full course, becomes worship.

From the earliest days of humanity, people have looked to the heavens to find meaning. Before telescopes, before science, before doctrines were penned and scriptures canonized, there was the sky. The ancients charted the stars not just for navigation or calendars, but as windows into the divine. The patterns of the constellations became stories, of gods and heroes, of purpose and destiny. The night sky was not a void; it was a cathedral.

Even today, in the age of satellites and simulations, when we understand so much more about what stars *are*, we are no less captivated by them. In fact, the more we learn, the more reverent we become. Science has not shrunk the mystery; it has magnified it.

The story begins with a bang. Or so we believe.

Roughly 13.8 billion years ago, the universe burst into existence from a single, unimaginably dense point, a singularity. This was the Big Bang: not an explosion in space, but the birth of space and time itself. From that one moment, every galaxy, every atom, every law of physics came into being. What was once nothing became everything. Darkness gave way to light. Chaos, somehow, gave rise to order.

Some see randomness in this. Others see the unmistakable fingerprints of a Creator. For what could be more divine than the act of creating all things out of nothing? The language of Genesis speaks of God saying, "Let there be light," and the universe obeying. The Big Bang does not contradict that, it echoes it. Both describe a moment when existence began, not by accident, but by will. And whether through sacred text or scientific theory, the message remains: there was a beginning, and it was no small thing.

Out of the superheated fog of that beginning, matter began to form. Hydrogen and helium coalesced under gravity's gentle but relentless pull. Clumps became clouds, clouds became stars. Deep in the hearts of these newborn stars, nuclear fusion ignited, turning simple elements into more complex ones: carbon, oxygen, nitrogen, iron. Every heavy element, every particle that would one day become trees and oceans and brains and hearts, was forged in the fire of stars.

When those stars exhausted their fuel, they died in spectacular fashion, supernovae that scattered their elemental treasures across the cosmos. These elements gathered again, forming planets, moons, comets, and eventually, us. It's not poetic exaggeration. It's scientific truth: *you are made of star stuff.*

But more than that, you are made *for wonder.*

We are not the cold byproducts of blind chance. We are the only known beings in the universe capable of looking up at the stars and asking, *Why?* That question itself is a form of worship. It arises from the soul's longing to connect with something beyond itself, something transcendent. To see the sky not as distant and indifferent, but as sacred.

This is where awe becomes holy.

To consider that the same forces that shape galaxies also knit together the fabric of our being is to glimpse unity in the vastness. The gravitational constants, the delicate balance of expansion and collapse, the precise tuning that allows stars to shine for billions of years, all of it speaks of intelligence, of artistry, of purpose.

The ancients worshipped because they saw the stars as divine. We worship today because we see the divine behind the stars.

Even in modern spiritual practice, many find God not in stained glass or sermons, but in stillness beneath the sky. There is a contemplative spirituality, ancient and yet utterly contemporary, that sees night not as darkness, but as invitation. Monks once prayed the Liturgy of the Hours by the phases of the moon. Nomadic tribes told sacred stories by starlight. Today, astrophotographers, poets, and seekers all pause beneath constellations to remember how small they are, and how deeply seen.

Because awe doesn't just humble us. It awakens us.

It reminds us that mystery is not our enemy, it is our home. That there are things we may never fully understand, and that's okay. In fact, that's where faith lives: not in having all the answers, but in allowing the unanswered to become sacred space.

Every orbit, every supernova, every delicate balance of light and gravity, declares not only that the universe is beautiful, but that it was made by Beauty itself.

And yet, there remains the paradox.

We are infinitesimal. Dust in the vastness. A breath in cosmic time. And still, we matter. The same God who commands quasars and black holes is intimately concerned with your heart. The One who shaped stars is shaping you. This duality, the grandeur of the cosmos and the tenderness of divine attention, is perhaps the deepest mystery of all.

To stare into the heavens and feel small is natural. To feel *loved* while feeling small is divine.

So let us not rush to explain away the stars. Let us not shrink the universe to something merely functional. Let it remain vast. Let it remain wild and mysterious and deep. For it is in that vastness that awe is born. And it is through awe that worship becomes not just an act, but a way of seeing, a way of living, a way of being.

When we allow the stars to speak, we remember that we are not alone. That the same breath that called galaxies into being still whispers within us.

And maybe, just maybe, the universe was not only designed *for* us, but *with* us in mind.

V. The Question of Life Beyond Earth

As we lift our eyes to the heavens, one question has echoed across generations, whispered in observatories and sanctuaries alike: *Are we alone?* Is this intricate choreography of life unique to Earth, or is it just one movement in a grander, cosmic symphony still unfolding in distant solar systems?

Astronomy has shown us that Earth is not the center of the universe. We are one planet orbiting one star among an estimated hundred billion in the Milky Way alone, and there are possibly two trillion galaxies beyond that. It is no longer a matter of whether Earth is rare, but how rare life itself might be. Astronomers have already discovered thousands of exoplanets, many orbiting their stars in the so-called *Goldilocks zones*, where conditions may support life. Water, the essential ingredient for biology as we know it, may be more widespread than we once imagined.

This does not diminish the wonder of Earth; it amplifies the wonder of creation. If God chose to populate other worlds with life, whether microbial or intelligent, carbon-based or something utterly unknown, would that not also proclaim His glory?

Christianity, contrary to some assumptions, does not demand Earthly exclusivity. The Bible is not a textbook of astronomy, but a revelation of relationship, God and humanity, Creator and creation. And while Scripture focuses on Earth because that is where the drama of redemption unfolds, it does not limit God's creative activity to this one sphere.

In fact, the psalmist declares, *"The heavens declare the glory of God..."* not *"this Earth alone."* The apostle Paul writes in Colossians 1:16 that *"through Him all things were created: things in heaven and on earth, visible and invisible... all things have been created through Him and for Him."* These are sweeping, cosmic statements. They do not suggest a timid God confined to a single planet. They speak of a boundless, imaginative Creator whose joy may well extend into galaxies we've yet to glimpse.

And yet the question grows more tender, more profound: *If intelligent life exists elsewhere, what of salvation?* Did Christ's death and resurrection on Earth affect only us? Would God incarnate again on another world, under another sun? We cannot know for certain, but neither should we fear the question.

C.S. Lewis, a devout Christian and one of the most thoughtful theological voices of the 20th century, addressed this idea in several of his works. In his *Space Trilogy*, he imagined planets untouched by sin, still in harmony with their Maker. He once wrote that if God did choose to redeem other races, "there might be other Incarnations," just as there are "other kinds of life." In other words, God's love is not bound by the limits of our sky. It is infinitely adaptable, endlessly creative, and eternally personal.

What we do know is this: the universe is vast not to make us feel irrelevant, but to reveal something of the vastness of God's love. If life exists elsewhere, it does not threaten faith, it expands it. It invites us to trust that the same God who knows the number of hairs on our head also knows the orbits of unseen worlds, and the hearts, if there are hearts, of beings we have not yet met.

And if, in all that endless expanse, we *are* alone, then it deepens the mystery: Why this world? Why us? Why such care, such intentionality, for this small blue dot?

Either way, the answer is awe.

Reflective Questions

When was the last time you looked at the stars and felt something stir inside you?

_____

_____

_____

_____

Does the precision of the cosmos make you feel more accidental or more chosen?

_____

_____

_____

_____

What does it mean to you that the same God who designed galaxies also designed you?

_____

_____

_____

_____

Chapter 7
Geology, the Creation of Earth, and Divine Purpose

"From the Source flows the light—into DNA, into breath, into soul. All of creation receives and reflects the Son."

I. Sacred Ground

What lies beneath us is not merely earth and rock, but the enduring memory of creation, etched in molten seams, hardened in time, and quietly bearing witness to a God who shapes not only souls, but planets. We walk every day across ground we rarely pause to contemplate, and yet, this earth, the dust that clings to our shoes, the rock that holds up our homes, the soil that nourishes our food, is nothing short of sacred. It is the stage upon which God's creative power unfurled across unimaginable epochs. It is the memory of the cosmos, held firm beneath our feet.

Science tells us that our planet formed over **4.54 billion years ago**, born from the swirling remains of exploding stars, particles gathering in a celestial dance of gravity and heat. Through violent collisions, molten chaos, and the slow cooling of a newborn crust, Earth came into being. It is a history etched in the deepest rock formations and the quiet rhythms of plate tectonics, those shifting, grinding forces beneath the surface that shape mountains, divide continents, and remind us how alive our planet truly is.

And yet, even amid this staggering scientific narrative, faith gives us language for awe that numbers alone cannot hold. We believe this Earth is not random, not accidental, but intentional. Crafted. Blessed. "In the beginning God created the heavens and the earth" (Genesis 1:1) not as an abstract idea but as a physical, tangible, life-giving body that still pulses with divine rhythm. This is no lifeless ball of minerals; it is a vessel of purpose.

Geology, with its relentless pursuit of truth through strata and sediment, does not contradict that purpose; it reveals it. It tells us that Earth's outer crust, which floats atop a molten mantle, is broken into **around 15 major tectonic plates**. These plates move mere centimeters each year, yet their movements have formed entire mountain ranges and opened vast oceanic basins. Isn't it wondrous that something so seemingly slow and invisible is behind some of the most dramatic expressions of nature? Scripture says, *"He set the earth on its foundations; it can never be moved"* (Psalm 104:5). This is not a contradiction, it is a poetic truth embedded within physical law. God is the author of both the verse and the volcano.

When we dig into the ground, we dig into memory. **Zircon crystals**, found in the Jack Hills of Western Australia, are **4.4 billion years old**, the oldest materials on Earth. These are the remnants of Earth's infancy, tiny gems forged under heat and pressure, bearing witness to a time before life began. And still, through science, we read their age. Through faith, we understand their origin. They are not just ancient, they are intentional.

To believe in a divine purpose is not to deny tectonics, mineralogy, or the cooling of a molten planet. Rather, it is to say: *"Even in all of this...especially in all of this...I see the hand of God."* The Creator is not absent from the processes but intimately intertwined into them, as present in the slow creep of magma beneath the crust as in the stillness of a prayer.

In this chapter, we will walk between the areas of geology and scripture, not to choose between them, but to see how they point together to something greater. We will descend into the rock, into the timeline of Earth, and rise with a renewed vision: that the ground beneath our feet is holy, and that every geological layer is another line in God's living, breathing manuscript.

Let us tread gently and reverently, for we are walking on sacred ground.

II. The Birth of a Planet:

The Earth is approximately **4.54 billion years old**, a fact confirmed through radiometric dating and the study of ancient meteorites. But it was not born in isolation. It came into being alongside the sun and other planets in a sequence of majestic, explosive processes. But behind this remarkable process, faith sees not just random chance, but divine arrangement. The **solar nebula**, from which all the planets emerged, was no accident, it was the raw canvas upon which the Creator would sculpt life. Scientists believe that the **solar system formed from the gravitational collapse of a region within a giant molecular cloud**. Imagine an immense, cold fog of hydrogen and helium stretching across light-years, suddenly disturbed, perhaps by the shockwave of a nearby supernova. That disturbance compressed part of the cloud, triggering it to collapse under its own gravity.

At the center of this collapse, pressure and heat built until **nuclear fusion ignited**, and the sun was born. The remaining material, dust and gas, continued swirling around the young star in a vast, spinning disk. Within this disk, particles began sticking together in a process known as **accretion**, much like how God slowly formed Adam from dust, small, simple pieces drawn together by unseen force until form became function, and function held the promise of life. Tiny grains collided and fused, slowly growing into larger and larger bodies, from pebbles to boulders, from boulders to planetesimals, rocky bodies many kilometers wide.

These planetesimals, through repeated collisions, eventually formed what we call **protoplanets**, including the early Earth. But Earth's creation was far from peaceful. The young solar system was a turbulent place, with frequent, high-energy impacts. The most significant of these collisions was with a Mars-sized body known as **Theia**. The impact was so violent that it vaporized part of Earth's crust and flung enormous amounts of debris into orbit. That debris eventually coalesced to form the **Moon**. This **giant impact hypothesis** is supported by isotopic similarities between lunar and terrestrial rocks, suggesting they share a common origin. You see, even in cosmic violence, the hand of God brings forth beauty and balance.

This process of creation echoes what is written in Genesis: "The earth was formless and empty, and darkness was over the surface of the deep" (Genesis 1:2). Out of formlessness came form. From celestial dust, a world fit for life was made. To look upon this scientific narrative is not to diminish God, but to stand in awe of His majesty, to see how even billions of years serve His timing.

After Earth formed, it remained a molten sphere for millions of years. **Temperatures inside early Earth likely exceeded 2000°C**, driven by the immense energy of accretion, frequent collisions, and radioactive decay. Imagine a glowing orb of iron and rock spinning in space, its surface shimmering with heat, erupting with geysers of lava, gas, and steam. It was uninhabitable. Lifeless. A crucible of chaos. And yet, within that searing heat, God's order was already at work.

As Earth slowly cooled, a process known as **planetary differentiation** began. This was not unlike the separation that happens when oil and water settle in a jar. Heavier elements, like iron and nickel, sank inward to form the **core**, while lighter elements rose toward the surface. This created a structured interior: a dense, metallic **inner core**, a swirling liquid **outer core**, a solid **mantle** of hot rock, and eventually, a thin **crust**, the surface we now walk on.

This stratification was not just physical, it was providential. The **iron core** generates Earth's **magnetic field**, which shields us from harmful solar radiation. The **mantle** carries heat upward through convection, driving the movement of Earth's surface plates. The **crust**, though fragile in comparison, contains the minerals, soils, and stability necessary for ecosystems and human civilization. In every layer, there is a kind of divine architecture: a blueprint not just for a planet, but for possibility.

It is here we see God's foresight in physical form. Much like the way the human body was knit together in the womb (Psalm 139:13), the Earth was also being formed in layers, each one essential, each one intentional. As the molten rock cooled and hardened, it did so not as an accident of heat, but as an act of divine precision. This was preparation, holy ground in the making.

As Earth cooled further, its crust solidified into plates, massive slabs of rock floating atop the semi-fluid mantle. The outer shell of Earth, known as the **lithosphere**, broke into about **15 major tectonic plates**. These plates are constantly shifting, slowly, almost imperceptibly, at rates of just **2 to 15 centimeters per year**, but over millions of years, they rearrange the continents, form mountains, and trigger earthquakes.

The first signs of this **plate tectonic activity** date back to about **3.2 billion years ago**, during the Archean Eon. This process has not only shaped Earth's physical geography but also profoundly influenced its climate, ecosystems, and habitability.

Take, for instance, the **Himalayas**, formed around **50 million years ago** when the Indian plate collided with the Eurasian plate. That ongoing collision continues to lift the mountains today. These monumental ranges act like natural altars rising into the sky, their creation echoing God's power to mold the Earth over eons.

Faith compels us to see these forces not merely as natural, but as sacred. They are not chaotic; they are rhythmic. The same divine voice that said, *"Let there be light,"* also whispered across the mantle, *"Let there be mountains."* Even earthquakes and volcanoes, though terrifying, are part of this dynamic design, a living Earth that breathes, shifts, and renews itself.

Plate tectonics also regulate Earth's **carbon cycle**. Through the subduction of carbon-rich rocks and the release of volcanic gases, they help maintain a stable atmosphere and climate. Without this geological "breath," the Earth would either freeze or boil. Isn't it awe-inspiring that what we often perceive as chaos, an earthquake, a volcanic eruption, is actually part of a life-sustaining balance? Faith teaches us that all things work together for good (Romans 8:28); geology gives us the tools to see how.

But how do we know all of this? How can we measure time that stretches back billions of years when human history barely spans ten thousand?

The answer lies in the rocks themselves. The oldest minerals on Earth, **zircon crystals** found in the **Jack Hills of Western Australia**, have been dated to **4.4 billion years ago** using **uranium-lead radiometric dating**. This technique relies on the predictable decay of radioactive elements. Uranium, for example, slowly decays into lead at a fixed rate, like the ticking of a cosmic clock. By measuring the ratio of uranium to lead in a mineral, scientists can calculate its age with extraordinary precision.

Other dating methods, such as **potassium-argon dating**, have been used to date volcanic layers and understand the age of fossils and mountain ranges. These techniques reveal a story that spans not just millennia, but eons, a story of transformation, upheaval, and persistent renewal.

Radiometric dating doesn't replace divine truth, it illuminates it. It confirms that creation is not a static event but an ongoing process. The Earth was not spoken into being in a single instant and then left untouched. Rather, like a great symphony, it was composed over time, each note a geological layer, each crescendo a tectonic shift, each rest a quieting of magma and fire.

These techniques do not strip away wonder, they deepen it. For when we hold a rock and know that it has endured for billions of years, we are reminded of Isaiah 40:8: *"The grass withers and the flowers fall, but the word of our God endures forever."* Just as God's word is eternal, so too is the memory of His creation, etched into stone and time.

To understand the Earth's birth through geology is not to push God aside. It is to marvel at the *means* by which He chose to shape our world. It is to stand at the edge of a canyon and recognize not just erosion, but evidence of divine patience. It is to see the Earth not merely as matter, but as a message.

From the spinning of gas in the solar nebula to the grinding of tectonic plates, every process has played a role in forming a planet that is not only livable but breathtakingly complex. God could have made the Earth instantly, but instead, He chose to work through time, through physics, through fire and stone. That choice speaks of a God who does not rush, who honors process, who writes His will not only in scripture, but in sediment and strata.

And as we stand today on the solid ground of a world that has endured heat, impact, and upheaval, we do so with reverence. This Earth is old. It is resilient. And above all, it is loved into being.

III. Geological Timescale and the Story of Life

If the Earth is the canvas of creation, then time is its slow, deliberate brushstroke. Every inch of rock beneath our feet is not merely stone, it is testimony. Testimony of a God who writes not just in ink or flame but in fossils, layers, sediments, and stardust. The geological timescale is not cold data, it is a living chronicle of a planet that was designed not only to exist, but to host, nurture, and eventually breathe with life.

This story of life is vast, spanning billions of years, and yet, within that immensity, we find something intimate: the fingerprints of God, delicately guiding evolution, adaptation, and renewal.

The history of the Earth is divided into **four grand eons**: **Hadean**, **Archean**, **Proterozoic**, and **Phanerozoic**, each an era of transformation, trial, and divine intention. These names may sound distant, but they represent the chapters of Earth's becoming, a sacred unfolding.

Hadean Eon (4.6–4.0 billion years ago)

Named after "Hades," this was a time of unimaginable heat and chaos. Earth was still in its infancy, volcanic, unstable, constantly bombarded by meteorites. There were no continents, no oceans, no atmosphere as we know it. It was a fiery crucible. And yet, even here, in what looked like unrelenting destruction, the conditions for life were being laid.

This was God preparing the clay.

Archean Eon (4.0–2.5 billion years ago)

During this time, the Earth cooled. Oceans formed. The skies darkened and cleared. Most miraculously, **life began**. In the shallow waters of primordial Earth, the first organisms, **simple, single-celled life** began to appear. These were **stromatolites**, microbial colonies that left layered, rock-like structures we can still find today in places like Shark Bay, Australia.

These were not complex beings, but they were alive...*alive*. Imagine that: cells breathing out oxygen long before the first tree stretched skyward, before lungs, blood, or even bones. They whispered the first signs of life into the atmosphere.

For the faithful, this is the moment where Genesis 1:2 begins to echo again: *"And the Spirit of God was hovering over the waters."* Indeed, God was not absent in these first glimmers of biology. He was already moving.

Proterozoic Eon (2.5 billion–541 million years ago)

Here, oxygen began to accumulate in Earth's atmosphere in what scientists call the **Great Oxygenation Event**. It was a long, slow process, but it forever changed Earth's chemistry, setting the stage for complex life.

This was the age of cellular evolution, when **eukaryotes**, cells with nuclei, appeared. This change opened the path for multicellular life. Picture the Creator sowing invisible seeds into the ocean's depths, cells communicating, clustering, forming primitive tissues and structures.

In Isaiah 55:10–11, it is written, *"As the rain and the snow come down from heaven, and do not return to it without watering the earth... so is my word that goes out from my mouth: it will not return to me empty."*

Life itself was that word, sent into the void, growing silently, obediently, purposefully.

Phanerozoic Eon (541 million years ago–present)

This is the eon we live in, and it begins with a miracle. Around **541 million years ago**, during the **Cambrian Explosion**, there was a sudden and rapid diversification of life. **Multicellular organisms** blossomed into forms that included **arthropods, mollusks, worms, corals, and the earliest vertebrates**.

It's as if the Earth took a deep breath and began to sing. Life surged. Not haphazardly, but in patterns. In relationships. In ecosystems.

And so began the long, astonishing climb toward the modern world: the rise of fish, amphibians, reptiles, birds, mammals, and eventually, humanity.

God, who had been painting with geology, began sculpting with life.

To walk in the desert and pick up a stone that holds a trilobite, a creature that lived hundreds of millions of years ago, is to hold memory itself. Fossils are not relics; they are scripture in stone. They are whispers from lives long gone, written in calcium and sediment.

Trilobites, with their segmented bodies and compound eyes, ruled the oceans of the Paleozoic era.

Ammonites, curled like ancient fingerprints, swam in prehistoric seas during the Mesozoic.

Dinosaurs, both gentle and terrible, roamed lush forests, plains, and swamps for more than 160 million years.

And then they were gone.

This Earth has not only seen life, it has seen death, extinction, and renewal. Scientists have identified **five major mass extinction events**, and among them:

- The **Permian-Triassic Extinction** (~252 million years ago) wiped out over 90% of marine species.

- The **Cretaceous-Paleogene Extinction** (~66 million years ago), caused by an asteroid impact, ended the reign of the dinosaurs and made space for mammals to rise.

These events were tragic, and yet, in the wake of each, new life emerged. Ferns after fire. Mammals after reptiles. Forests after floods.

To the faithful heart, this is not simply biological turnover. It is divine regeneration. *"Behold, I make all things new,"* God declares in Revelation 21:5. The Earth, too, obeys this rhythm, of dying and rising, of shedding and renewing.

Even in extinction, there is grace. Even in silence, there is preparation for song.

We also often forget that all life depends not just on water or air, but on soil. That humble brown layer underfoot is holy. It is the result of **millions of years** of geological weathering, biological decay, and microbial cooperation.

Soil began to form when rocks, exposed to wind, rain, and early plant roots, began to **break down**. Over time, decaying organisms enriched this mineral base with organic matter, giving us **topsoil**, that thin, vital veil where food is grown, forests are rooted, and civilizations rise.

But the process is slow. It can take **500 years** to create just **one inch of healthy topsoil**.

Even here, God's patience is evident.

Within every gram of soil live **billions of microbes**, bacteria, fungi, archaea, all working together to cycle nutrients, retain moisture, and support plant growth. These microbes form the **foundation of the food chain**, quietly sustaining all visible life.

Jesus said, *"Unless a grain of wheat falls into the earth and dies, it remains alone; but if it dies, it bears much fruit."* (John 12:24)

Soil is the vessel of this promise. Everything that dies, leaves, insects, even our ancestors, returns to it. And from it, new life rises. The **humus** in soil shares its root word with **humility**, a reminder that all things return to the earth, and that creation, at its core, is cyclical and sacred.

Soil is not mere dirt, it is a living tabernacle. It is where God plants His promises.

The geological timescale may seem abstract, billions of years, strange names, slow processes. But taken together, it is a profound testament to divine craftsmanship. It is not in opposition to faith, it *is* faith, seen in layers. It reveals a God who does not rush but who builds slowly, lovingly, with attention to detail.

It shows us:

- That **life began in simplicity**, and was never beneath God's care.

- That **extinction and renewal** are not ends, but transitions under heaven's watch.

- That **soil, fossils, and the rocks beneath our feet** are part of an unfolding story still being written.

And we, as part of that story, must learn to read the Earth not just with microscopes and maps, but with reverence. With gratitude. With awe.

In every layer, from ancient stromatolites to rich farmland, we find a quiet, enduring message:

You are standing on sacred ground.

This is not just Earth.

This is Creation.

IV. Creation and Divine Purpose

As the dust of stars gave rise to oceans and mountains, valleys and winds, so too does our religion look to these physical realities not as accidents but as *intention*. The rocks cry out with history. The Earth pulses with order. The movements of tectonic plates, the balance of atmospheric gases, the carbon cycles and oxygen-rich oceans, none of this is chaos. None of it is meaningless. Rather, it all points to a Creator whose imagination is matched only by His precision.

Theology does not flinch before geology. On the contrary, it embraces it as the long arc of divine purpose working through time.

The very first words of Scripture thunder with cosmic weight: *"In the beginning, God created the heavens and the earth."* (Genesis 1:1)

What follows in Genesis 1 is not merely myth or poetry, it is a sequence of ordered, intentional acts. Light is called forth, "Let there be light," before the sun is even named. This divine utterance mirrors, in remarkable symbolic resonance, the scientific model of the **Big Bang**, where light burst into being and energy condensed into matter, marking time's first tick. The universe did not stumble into existence; it *began*.

Day by day, structure was added: sky from waters, land from sea, plants, stars, creatures, each layered like sediment, each called "good."

Psalm 104 deepens this revelation, offering a poetic but detailed image of God's ongoing creative activity:

"He makes springs pour water into the ravines; it flows between the mountains. They give water to all the beasts of the field... He makes grass grow for the cattle, and plants for people to cultivate, bringing forth food from the earth." (Psalm 104:10–14)

This is not a remote deity casting the cosmos from a distance. This is a *God of process*, a God of geology, ecology, and biology, co-authoring with time.

Even Job, in his moment of despair, was redirected by God toward the Earth's grandeur:

"Where were you when I laid the Earth's foundation?... Who marked off its dimensions? Surely you know!" (Job 38:4–5)

Creation is not an afterthought in theology, it is the first testament of God's nature.

Among the billions of planets in the galaxy, Earth occupies a place so particular, so finely tuned for life, that it evokes not just scientific interest but spiritual awe.

Earth lies in what scientists call the **habitable zone**, the "Goldilocks zone" neither too hot nor too cold. Positioned **93 million miles** from the sun, its orbit is stable and nearly circular, avoiding extreme temperatures that would sterilize the planet.

Its **atmosphere**, a delicate balance of nitrogen and oxygen, not only allows respiration but filters harmful solar radiation. The presence of **liquid water**, stable for billions of years, is not a common trait among planets; it is a cosmic gift.

Even more miraculous is the Earth's **magnetic field**, generated by the spinning of its **molten iron core**, which protects us from solar wind and cosmic radiation. Without it, the atmosphere would have been stripped away long ago, as happened on Mars.

The slow churn of **tectonic plates** helps recycle carbon through the atmosphere and mantle, maintaining long-term **climate stability**, a critical factor in sustaining complex life.

This elegant coordination led the late Christian physicist **John Polkinghorne** to write: *"The universe is not just a place where we happen to live. It is a place perfectly suited for the emergence of life, and ultimately, of consciousness. It is not an accident."*

This is the doctrine of **fine-tuning**, and for many believers, it reads not as scientific coincidence but divine invitation. Creation is not simply *that which was made*, but *that which was made for us*.

Christian thinkers throughout history have wrestled with the relationship between creation and Creator. Far from seeing science and faith as enemies, many saw nature as a sacred manuscript.

St. Augustine of Hippo famously taught that creation was like a second book, a text that, like Scripture, revealed truths about God. To misread creation, or ignore its evidence, was to misread the author.

"Some people, in order to discover God, read a book. But there is a greater book: the very appearance of created things. Look above you! Look below

you! Read it. God whom you want to discover never wrote that book with ink. Instead, He set before your eyes the things that He had made."

Pierre Teilhard de Chardin, both a Jesuit priest and a paleontologist, saw evolution as the very method of divine action. To him, geological processes were not void of God, they *were* the unfolding of God's will through deep time. He famously wrote:

"Evolution is not opposed to faith. It demands faith, a faith of cosmic scope."

For Chardin, the Earth's long history of transformation, its plates, species, and extinctions, was a sacred journey toward increasing complexity, beauty, and eventually, consciousness. It was the world's *pilgrimage to the divine.*

This is not sentimentalism. It is theological courage. It is the willingness to see God not just in miracles but in *magma*, in *mineral*, in *mutation*.

The psalmist declared:

"The heavens declare the glory of God; the skies proclaim the work of His hands." (Psalm 19:1)

And yet, the Earth declares too. Mountains and valleys, fossil beds and fault lines, all are verses in the terrestrial hymn.

Geology, to the faithful mind, is not just a science, it is **revelation through matter**. Each layer of rock is a **testament of time**, a memory preserved. The granite cliffs of Yosemite, carved by glaciers; the Grand Canyon, etched by the Colorado River; the volcanic arches of Iceland, they are cathedrals of time and pressure.

To stand before them is to stand in awe, not of impersonal forces, but of divine artistry.

Rocks are **witnesses**. Mountains, in their grandeur and age, speak of **God's endurance**. Fossils, fragile and buried, whisper of **God's attentiveness to even the smallest life**. Geology becomes not just evidence of how the Earth formed, but *why it formed*.

Yet geology is not always peaceful. Earthquakes, volcanoes, and tsunamis remind us that creation is not static, it is dynamic, and at times, dangerous.

A magnitude-9 earthquake releases more energy than all the nuclear weapons ever tested. The 2004 Indian Ocean tsunami took over 230,000 lives. Volcanic eruptions have blocked out the sun and altered climate for years at a time.

To many, these events challenge belief: *How can a good God permit such upheaval?*

But faith traditions have long wrestled with suffering and fragility, not to dismiss them, but to interpret them. Scripture calls us not to arrogance, but **humility**:

"All people are like grass, and all their glory is like the flowers of the field." (Isaiah 40:6)

Geology reminds us that we are **temporary tenants** of a very old planet. We are not in control, but we are *invited to steward*. The violence of Earth is not divine punishment but the price of its liveliness. Tectonic activity, while destructive, is also what keeps the Earth habitable over eons. Without earthquakes, we wouldn't have mountains or mineral cycles. Even in chaos, there is **purpose**.

If geology teaches us the Earth is ancient, fragile, and rare, then theology calls us to **protect it**.

"The Lord God took the man and put him in the Garden of Eden to work it and take care of it." (Genesis 2:15)

This command is not revoked by modernity. It grows more urgent. We are the first generation capable of **mapping the planet's deep time**, but also the first generation capable of **unraveling its ecological balance**.

Fossil fuels, born of ancient biomass, have powered our growth, but also threaten our future. Mining has unearthed vital resources, and scarred landscapes. Water tables are being depleted. Forests are falling.

Christian ethics must meet geology with **stewardship, not exploitation**.

In his 2015 encyclical *Laudato Si'*, Pope Francis issued a prophetic call:

"The Earth, our home, is beginning to look more and more like an immense pile of filth."

And yet, he calls for **ecological conversion**, a change in heart, not just practice. He writes that the Earth is not a commodity but a **sister**, and that our duty is to "hear both the cry of the Earth and the cry of the poor."

When Jesus entered Jerusalem, the crowd praised Him. The Pharisees urged Him to quiet them. He replied:

"I tell you, if they keep quiet, the stones will cry out." (Luke 19:40)

The stones still cry. With heat, pressure, and time, they declare the patience of God. With fossils, they testify to His creativity. With eruptions and erosion, they reveal both His power and our vulnerability.

Geology is not anti-faith. It is **ancient scripture**, written not in Hebrew or Greek but in granite and coal, fossil and fault line.

159

To study geology faithfully is to read this deeper book, to listen for the long, quiet voice of the Creator who not only spoke light into being, but who *continues to speak through stone.*

V. Bridging Science and Faith

In every era, a false tension has risen between science and belief, as if understanding the mechanics of creation could erase the need for a Creator. But this is not a conflict born of truth; it is a fracture born of misunderstanding.

Science reveals. Faith interprets. One investigates how. The other seeks why. They are not enemies, but companions, two ways of reading the same story, written across the heavens and etched into the Earth.

Some of the most profound voices in both theology and science have echoed this compatibility, not as a compromise, but as a harmony.

Dr. Francis Collins, a physician-geneticist and former Director of the National Institutes of Health, led the Human Genome Project, mapping the intricacies of our genetic code. Yet he is also a devout Christian and the founder of **BioLogos**, an organization dedicated to showing that science and biblical faith can coexist without contradiction.

"Science is not the enemy of faith," Collins writes. "It is, instead, a means of getting a glimpse of God's mind."

For Collins and many like him, the study of Earth's age, its structure, and its long geological narrative does not challenge the faith, it deepens it. Knowing that the Earth is **4.54 billion years old**, that tectonic processes began over **3 billion years ago**, and that life has evolved through struggle and transformation, only makes creation more majestic, not less.

160

The **Vatican Observatory**, one of the oldest astronomical research institutions in the world, has long supported this synthesis. Its scientists, many of whom are Jesuit priests, engage in astrophysics, planetary science, and geology not in spite of their belief in God, but because of it. They see scientific exploration as a form of *praise*.

Pope John Paul II once stated:

"Science can purify religion from error and superstition; religion can purify science from idolatry and false absolutes."

Together, they help humanity to grasp both the grandeur of the cosmos and the dignity of creation.

Some of the most influential geologists in history have approached their work not only with academic rigor but also with reverence.

Take **James Dwight Dana**, a Yale professor and pioneering 19th-century geologist. Dana studied volcanoes, earthquakes, and the structure of continents. But he also wrote passionately about divine order within Earth's processes. He did not see geology as a threat to God's authority, but as a *window into it*.

Or consider **David Montgomery**, a modern-day geomorphologist who studies how landscapes evolve. Though raised in a secular environment, Montgomery came to appreciate the spiritual dimension of geology. In his book *"The Rocks Don't Lie: A Geologist Investigates Noah's Flood"*, he acknowledges that geology doesn't debunk faith, it corrects literalism while preserving the deeper truths of moral and spiritual insight.

For both men and for countless others, the Earth is not just a planet of plate boundaries and stratified rocks. It is **holy**

ground, shaped by physical forces but infused with **mystery and meaning**.

Their common posture is **humility**…humility before deep time, before planetary scale, and before the realization that we are small but not insignificant. We are, as the Psalmist says, *"fearfully and wonderfully made,"* set upon an Earth sculpted by fire, water, and time.

This humility is itself theological. It is the recognition that while we cannot fully comprehend the vastness of Earth's history, we can stand in awe of it, grateful for the minds to study it and the hearts to revere it.

Beneath our feet lies more than rock and soil. Beneath our feet lies a **story, 4.5 billion years long**, layered in sediment, written in tectonics, colored by magma and clay. This is the ground that once birthed volcanoes and split supercontinents. This is the same ground that now cradles gardens, cities, cathedrals, and the bones of those who came before us.

Geology tells us that the Earth has known **catastrophe and renewal**, extinction and abundance. It has been frozen and scorched, fractured and healed. Its mountains have risen and crumbled, its oceans have advanced and receded. And through it all, life has persisted, guided, it would seem, not merely by chance, but by providence.

To look at the Earth geologically is to gaze into **deep time**, to see that we are recent visitors to an ancient home. But to look at the Earth through the eyes of faith is to see that **even stone carries divine fingerprints**.

The story of geology is not at odds with faith, it is saturated with it.

When the ground trembles with earthquakes or sings with the silence of a desert plain, when a fossilized fern is uncovered or a crystal formation is admired, we are witnessing not just nature, we are witnessing **revelation**.

This is sacred ground, not just because it sustains us, but because it **reveals** the One who sustains it.

The Earth is not simply a place we live. It is a story we inherit, a story etched in rock, encoded in soil, told by stars and rivers and layers of ancient dust. And if we listen closely, we may hear it speak, not only of time and science, but of **God**, who shaped the stars and spoke light into being, who formed the land and called it good.

We walk, each day, not merely upon rock, but upon a **holy manuscript**, one written long before us, but meant for us to read.

And in reading it, we worship.

Reflective Questions

What stirs in you when you gaze upon the bones of mountains, the scars of earthquakes, the fossils of forgotten creatures? Is it fear, doubt, or reverence?

_____

_____

_____

_____

If the Earth took billions of years to become what it is, might your own becoming take time too? What grace lies in long formation?

_____

_____

_____

_____

How do you live upon this ancient Earth: as a visitor, a caretaker, or a child of both dust and divinity?

_____

_____

_____

_____

Chapter 8
Overcoming the Conflict Myth

Faith preserved knowledge.
Faith pursued knowledge.

I. Addressing the Idea that Science Disproves Faith

There's a certain mythology that lives quietly in our culture, a whisper turned dogma, that tells us we must choose between the microscope and the prayer, between the laboratory and the chapel. It's a story passed down with more conviction than evidence, shaped not by truth but by tension. This is the "science versus religion" narrative, a well-worn tale that suggests one must either believe in God or believe in gravity, never both.

But like many myths, this one is rooted more in conflict than clarity.

The formal seeds of this narrative were planted in the 19th century, particularly through the works of John William Draper and Andrew Dickson White. Draper, in his book *History of the Conflict Between Religion and Science*, and White, in *A History of the Warfare of Science with Theology in Christendom*, argued that religion had historically stood in the way of scientific progress. Their work gave rise to what historians now call the Conflict Thesis, the belief that religion and science have always been in opposition.

At first glance, the thesis feels plausible. After all, we've heard stories of brave scientists silenced by the church, of discoveries buried under fear of heresy. The image is cinematic. Galileo muttering *"Eppur si muove"* under his breath after recanting his support for heliocentrism. Giordano Bruno burned at the stake. These moments are burned into collective memory as emblems of faith's hostility toward truth.

But history, like people, is more complex than slogans allow.

Galileo's trial was as much about power and politics as theology. Bruno's execution was not solely for his scientific ideas but also for his pantheistic and theological positions, which challenged both Church authority and core Christian doctrine. Still, these tragic and dramatic moments have been

167

used to reinforce a black-and-white narrative: faith restricts; science liberates.

What gets lost in this binary, however, are the countless believers who were also seekers, who prayed and peered through telescopes in the same breath. From Isaac Newton, whose study of physics was intimately tied to his belief in divine order, to Georges Lemaître, the Catholic priest who proposed what would become known as the Big Bang theory, faith and science have coexisted not in opposition, but often in profound collaboration.

II. Misunderstandings about Scientific Methodology

Part of what fuels the conflict myth is a fundamental misunderstanding of what science is, and isn't.

Science is a method. A disciplined, rigorous, humble tool that allows us to ask questions about the natural world and seek answers through observation, experimentation, and evidence. It tells us how the planets move, how cells divide, how ecosystems balance, how stars are born. It is not, and was never meant to be, a philosophy of life. It is descriptive, not prescriptive.

Where confusion arises is when people begin to ask science to answer questions it was never designed to confront: Why am I here? What is the meaning of suffering? Is there life after death? Does love matter? Is there a God?

These are metaphysical and existential questions. They dwell in the domain of philosophy, ethics, theology, and spirituality. They speak not to how the world works, but why it matters. And while science can illuminate aspects of these mysteries, offering, for instance, neurological explanations for spiritual experiences or evolutionary theories of altruism, it cannot, by its very nature, declare a final word on meaning.

The late Stephen Jay Gould, a prominent evolutionary biologist and historian of science, coined the idea of Non-Overlapping Magisteria (NOMA) to describe this distinction. In Gould's view, science and religion occupy separate but complementary domains of teaching authority, or "magisteria." Science covers the empirical realm, what the universe is made of (fact) and why it works this way (theory). Religion deals with questions of ultimate meaning and moral value.

When one magisterium tries to do the job of the other, tension arises.

This is where the emotional disconnect comes in. We live in an age of measurable data and algorithmic certainty. We grow uncomfortable with uncertainty. We want proof, or at least predictability. So when someone says they believe in something they cannot see or test or reproduce, there's a cultural instinct to dismiss it as primitive, irrational, or obsolete.

But is it irrational to love? To hope? To mourn someone gone yet feel their presence? These are not testable experiences, yet they are among the most real parts of being human. Faith, in this way, is not a competitor to science, but an interpreter of all that lies beyond its reach.

III. Misuse of Science or Religion to Undermine the Other

While some of the conflict myth is born from misunderstanding, much of it is also sustained by deliberate misuse of both science and religion.

Let's begin with religion. There have been, undeniably, moments when religious institutions have rejected scientific findings out of fear or control. From persecuting early astronomers to resisting the theory of evolution, certain interpretations of faith have become rigid in ways that shut down inquiry.

This is religious fundamentalism at its most damaging: when belief becomes brittle and fearful, rather than resilient and curious.

But on the other side of the spectrum lies a different kind of rigidity, scientific materialism, which insists that only what can be measured is real, and that faith is mere superstition. This worldview often presents itself as enlightened, progressive, and superior, but it can be just as dismissive and dogmatic.

Take Richard Dawkins, for example, who once described belief in God as a "delusion," equating it to belief in a teapot orbiting the sun. While such provocations spark headlines, they rarely leave room for nuance or dialogue. They reduce the rich, complex experience of faith to a caricature and shut the door on any conversation that dares to blend wonder with evidence.

The misuse of science to attack religion often pretends to be neutral, but it carries the same kind of fervor once used by inquisitors, only now in defense of secularism. And the irony is not lost: the tools meant to liberate thought are sometimes wielded to silence belief.

The answer isn't to dismiss science or faith, but to recognize the danger in absolutism. Both science and religion, when twisted to serve ideology or power, can become harmful. But in their purest forms, they ask the same thing of us: humility. To admit how little we know. To marvel at what we can discover. To dare to believe there's more to reality than we can fully grasp.

And it's worth returning to those stories often used as weapons in this debate.

Galileo Galilei's conflict with the Catholic Church is perhaps the most cited example of science and religion at odds. In 1633, Galileo was tried by the Inquisition for advocating heliocentrism, the idea that the Earth revolves around the sun. He was forced to recant and lived under house arrest for the rest of his life.

It's a heartbreaking story. But what's often left out is that many within the Church supported scientific inquiry. The issue was less about heliocentrism and more about who had the authority to interpret scripture and truth. The Church felt threatened not by the telescope, but by the theological implications of shifting the Earth from the center of the universe.

Galileo himself was a man of faith. He wrote of God as the creator of nature and scripture alike. "The Bible tells us how to go to heaven, not how the heavens go," he famously said. His life is not a cautionary tale of choosing science over faith, but a plea to let both speak.

Giordano Bruno is often presented as a martyr for science, but his story, too, is complex. A Dominican friar, philosopher, and mathematician, Bruno proposed that the universe was infinite and filled with many worlds. But his ideas were deeply mystical and theological, not strictly scientific. He held controversial views on the soul, reincarnation, and the nature of divinity that challenged both Catholic and Protestant doctrine.

His execution in 1600 was brutal and unjust, but it was not solely because of scientific views, it was for heresy. To reduce Bruno's death to a science-vs-religion clash is to flatten a profound and painful story into a propaganda tool.

The truth is this: the world is full of people who believe in both the Big Bang and Genesis, who study evolutionary biology and still bow their heads in prayer, who decode DNA while believing it was written by a Creator.

The most profound discoveries of science, like the fine-tuning of the universe, the complexity of the human brain, or the origins of consciousness, often stir, rather than silence, spiritual awe. Scientists like Francis Collins, who led the Human Genome Project and is an outspoken Christian, see their work not as a replacement for belief but as a way to deepen it.

We don't need to pit curiosity against conviction. We don't need to choose between reason and reverence.

Instead, we can recognize that science and faith are both expressions of a uniquely human longing to understand the world, and to find our place within it. One examines what is. The other contemplates what it means. And both, in their own ways, point us toward wonder.

Misconceptions are powerful. They shape education, public policy, and even personal identity. But they are not unbreakable.

The conflict between science and faith is not an eternal truth, it is a story. And stories can be re-examined. Rewritten. Reclaimed.

What's needed now is honesty, humility, and the courage to listen, really listen, to both the scientist in her lab and the mystic in his chapel. Because when you clear away the noise and fear, you'll often find they are asking the same question, just in different languages:

What is this world? And why does it matter that we're here?

And maybe, just maybe, the answer lives in both the whisper of a prayer and the gleam of a telescope.

IV. The Role of Faith in Scientific Advancement

It is easy to forget that the roots of scientific inquiry were not grown in opposition to faith, but in its very soil. Many of the earliest scientists were not skeptics of religion but devoted believers. For them, the study of nature was not a means to escape God, but a method to draw closer to the divine. To understand creation was to honor the Creator. This profound harmony between faith and curiosity, between theology and theory, helped shape the scientific revolution and continues to inspire inquiry today.

At the heart of this relationship lies a foundational belief: that the universe is orderly, rational, and knowable, because it was created by a God who is orderly, rational, and knowable.

This was no small assumption. In a world where ancient mythologies described nature as chaotic and arbitrarily ruled by capricious gods whose tempers shaped the tides and skies, the Judeo-Christian worldview introduced something revolutionary. It spoke of a universe that functioned according to laws, not whims; a cosmos that was not random, but designed. The very idea that one could study the stars, map the human body, or analyze the elements depended on the conviction that there was something consistent and intelligible to be studied.

This was a theological proposition before it became a scientific one.

Christianity in particular proposed that the universe was **not divine**, but **created**, and therefore separate from God, worthy of examination and understanding. Unlike belief systems that saw nature as sacred and untouchable, the Christian view encouraged exploration. To investigate the natural world was not blasphemous; it was a form of worship.

Furthermore, the idea of humans made in the image of God (imago Dei) imbued humanity with reason, creativity, and moral responsibility. If God had given us minds capable of understanding the world, it followed that using those minds to explore creation was part of our sacred duty. This theological underpinning provided not only the permission to study nature but the mandate.

That sense of purpose, rooted in belief, drove many early scientists. They did not see a wall between their faith and their investigations. They saw a bridge.

V. Patronage and Support of Science by Religious Institutions

In addition to theological encouragement, material support for scientific inquiry often came directly from religious institutions. Far from being antagonistic toward science, many monasteries, churches, and religious orders became centers of learning that preserved, taught, and advanced scientific knowledge.

During the so-called "Dark Ages," when much of Europe's classical knowledge risked being lost, monasteries became the great preservers of wisdom. Monks copied ancient manuscripts, maintained libraries, and studied natural phenomena. The Benedictine order, in particular, emphasized a balance of prayer and work, *ora et labora*, which included intellectual labor. Their gardens became laboratories. Their clocks marked not just liturgical hours, but astronomical observations.

These communities cultivated curiosity as a spiritual discipline.

One example is Isidore of Seville, a 7th-century bishop whose encyclopedic works preserved a wealth of classical scientific knowledge. In the Islamic world, religious scholars similarly safeguarded and expanded upon Greek, Roman, and Persian scientific texts, which would later return to Europe via translations preserved in monasteries and cathedral schools.

The Catholic Church, in particular, has a complex yet often misunderstood relationship with science. While infamous for certain conflicts, such as the Galileo affair, it also played a crucial role in advancing scientific disciplines, especially astronomy and medicine.

The Church's liturgical calendar and the calculation of Easter required precise astronomical knowledge, which led to ecclesiastical investment in star charts and planetary movements. Cathedrals were designed as solar observatories, and some even functioned as giant sundials. Clergy were often the best-educated individuals in a community and served as doctors, teachers, and scientists.

Figures like Roger Bacon, a 13th-century Franciscan friar, pioneered the experimental method long before it became formalized. He believed that understanding nature helped illuminate theological truths and insisted on observation and empirical reasoning as tools to deepen faith.

In medicine, religious orders ran the first hospitals in Europe. Monks and nuns cared for the sick, experimented with herbal treatments, and developed systems for medical education. While today medicine may seem secular, its roots are entwined with Christian care for the suffering.

One of the most enduring testaments to the Church's engagement with science is the Vatican Observatory, one of the oldest astronomical research institutions in the world. Founded in the late 16th century by Pope Gregory XIII, the observatory was established to reform the calendar, a project requiring precise astronomical calculation.

But it didn't stop there. Over the centuries, the Vatican Observatory has contributed to scientific discovery through stellar cataloging, spectroscopy, and meteorite research. Today, its scientists, many of them Jesuit priests, work with cutting-edge telescopes in Arizona and Castel Gandolfo. One of its current leaders, Brother Guy Consolmagno, holds degrees from MIT and speaks passionately about how studying the cosmos deepens his faith.

In this way, the Vatican Observatory stands as a luminous counter-narrative to the idea that religion fears science. Instead, it shows what's possible when belief and curiosity stand side by side.

VI. Modern Integration of Faith and Science

As we move into the 21st century, the perceived divide between science and faith continues to dissolve, not in theory alone, but in the lives of real people. Today, there are countless scientists whose research is driven not by a desire to disprove God, but by a profound sense of wonder, purpose, and reverence. These individuals see no contradiction in praying in the morning and peering through a microscope by afternoon.

Among the most notable is Dr. Francis Collins, the physician-geneticist who led the Human Genome Project, the monumental international effort to map the entire human genetic code. Collins is also a committed Christian who has written openly about his journey from atheism to faith in his book *The Language of God*. For Collins, the intricacy and elegance of DNA is not an argument against belief, but a form of divine speech, a sacred script written in the very language of biology.

Collins has said: "I see no conflict in being a rigorous scientist and a person who believes in a God who takes a personal interest in each one of us." His work exemplifies how scientific brilliance and spiritual conviction can exist not in tension, but in deep harmony.

Another powerful voice is Katharine Hayhoe, an atmospheric scientist and evangelical Christian. As one of the most respected voices in climate science, Hayhoe speaks passionately about the intersection of faith and environmental stewardship. She argues that caring for the Earth is a deeply moral and spiritual obligation, rooted in biblical teachings about creation care.

Then there is Brother Guy Consolmagno, the aforementioned Jesuit astronomer, who works at the Vatican Observatory. Known for his warmth and wit, Consolmagno frequently speaks about how his fascination with space points him toward God. "Religion needs science to keep it away from superstition," he says, "and science needs religion to keep it away from idolatry."

177

These testimonies aren't isolated cases. Studies show that a significant percentage of scientists, especially in the United States, hold religious beliefs. According to a Pew Research Center survey, around half of American scientists believe in some form of a higher power. While fewer may adhere to traditional religious practices, many express a sense of spiritual awe at the complexity and beauty of the universe.

In other words, belief and evidence are not mutually exclusive. They are often companions on the same path.

Recognizing the value of this integration, many academic institutions and organizations now actively promote dialogue between science and religion.

BioLogos, founded by Francis Collins, is one such organization. It brings together scientists, theologians, and laypeople to explore how modern science and biblical faith can enrich one another. The organization addresses controversial topics, such as evolution and genetics, without abandoning either theological integrity or scientific rigor.

The American Scientific Affiliation (ASA) is another example, a network of Christians in science who engage in scholarly discourse about the compatibility of faith and scientific discovery. Their work emphasizes humility, dialogue, and intellectual honesty.

In the UK, the Faraday Institute for Science and Religion, based at Cambridge University, offers research, publications, and educational programs that promote constructive engagement between theology and science. Named after Michael Faraday, a devout Christian and pioneering physicist, the institute embodies a long tradition of faith-inspired scientific pursuit.

These institutions represent a broader movement, an awakening of sorts, within academia. No longer must one check their faith at the laboratory door or leave their intellect outside the sanctuary. The two can meet, converse, and grow together.

Beyond formal institutions, there are everyday stories of scientists, doctors, and engineers whose lives reveal the compatibility of faith and science in practice.

They are the physicians who pray quietly before surgery. The astrophysicists who marvel at creation and feel moved to worship. The biologists who see the divine fingerprint in the complexity of ecosystems. The environmental scientists who cite scripture as the motivation for their conservation work.

Faith does not hinder their work, it deepens it.

In many fields, particularly medicine, genetics, and environmental science, theological reflection plays a critical role in shaping ethical practice. Questions of when life begins, how to handle end-of-life care, what boundaries should exist in gene editing, or how to respond to climate change are not merely technical questions. They are moral ones.

Science provides the tools. Faith offers the framework.

This is where theology becomes not just relevant but necessary. It reminds us that knowledge without wisdom can be dangerous. That power without purpose can harm. That just because we can do something does not always mean we should.

And so, the integration of faith and science continues, not as a compromise, but as a collaboration. As two ways of knowing that, when held together, help us see the world more fully, love it more deeply, and live within it more wisely.

History tells a story that is more complex and beautiful than the old myths allow. Faith has not only survived the rise of science, it has often given it wings. The belief in a rational Creator gave birth to the idea of a rational universe. The support of monasteries and religious orders nurtured the growth of science in its infancy. Today, scientists of faith continue to show us that the heart and the mind do not need to be in conflict.

We live in a world of wonder. We are beings of spirit and reason, of longing and logic. And perhaps the greatest discovery we can make is not in the stars or the strands of DNA, but in the realization that these two gifts, faith and science, were never meant to stand apart.

They are not adversaries.

They are companions.

And together, they help us touch the mystery of existence with both reverence and understanding.

Reflective Questions

Have you ever felt pressure to choose between being intellectually curious and being spiritually grounded? Why or why not?

_____

_____

_____

_____

Can you recall a moment when scientific discovery inspired awe or a deeper sense of the divine? What was it?

_____

_____

_____

_____

What role do I believe spiritual belief should, or shouldn't, play in public conversations about science and ethics?

_____

_____

_____

_____

Chapter 9
God is Love!

Love is the one force that both humbles us and elevates us. It softens the hardest hearts, revives the weary, and gives meaning to lives fractured by pain or isolation. From the first breath a newborn takes in its mother's arms to the last whispered goodbye between soulmates, love wraps itself around us, unseen, but deeply felt.

At its core, love is not merely a poetic ideal or a fleeting emotion; it is a force woven into the very structure of our humanity. Biologically, love sparks a cascade of neurochemical reactions that calm our fears and deepen our bonds. Psychologically, it becomes the foundation of trust, self-worth, and empathy. Socially, it stitches communities together, nurturing cooperation and resilience. And spiritually, it calls us to something higher, something eternal.

Christianity does not speak of love as an optional virtue or vague concept, it proclaims, *"God is love"* (1 John 4:8). These three simple words form the cornerstone of Christian theology and human hope. They declare that love is not just something God does; it is who God is. Every heartbeat of compassion, every act of sacrifice, every moment of tenderness is an echo of that divine origin.

In this chapter, we will explore how love transforms us from the inside out, how it reshapes our brains, heals our wounds, elevates our relationships, and calls our souls toward eternity. Through scientific studies, historical insights, and spiritual truths, we will discover that love is not a weakness, but our greatest power. And when grounded in faith, it becomes not just a human force, but a holy one.

I. The Biology of Love

Have you ever wondered what exactly happens inside us when we feel loved, truly, deeply loved? It's more than just a flutter in the stomach or a racing heart. Love has a language of its own, written not just in poems and promises, but in chemicals and currents pulsing through our very bodies.

The first time you hold someone's hand and feel your chest flutter. The way a parent cradles a newborn and the whole world feels sacred. The comfort of being listened to without judgment. These moments are soaked in chemistry. They aren't just emotional, they're biological.

Our brains, when flooded by love, release a potent blend of chemicals sometimes called the **"love cocktail."**

Recipe for Love Cocktail:

1. **Oxytocin (1 cup)**, released through physical touch and emotional connection, is often referred to as the "bonding hormone" or the "moral molecule." It makes us feel safe, promotes trust, and quiets fear.

2. **Dopamine (1/2 cup)**, the pleasure and reward chemical, gives us that spark of euphoria, that magnetic pull toward people who matter to us.

3. **Serotonin (1 tsp)** helps regulate mood and social behavior, anchoring us in calm and stability.

4. **Endorphins (2 tbsp)** bring about comfort, even euphoria, they're natural painkillers, soothing both body and soul.

These chemicals don't just make us feel good, they rewire the brain. They teach us, over time, what safety, trust, and love feel like. And once we've tasted them, we long to return.

Dr. Helen Fisher, a leading expert in the neuroscience of love, conducted fMRI studies in the early 2000s that showed what the brain looks like when someone is in love. When subjects looked at photos of their romantic partners, regions rich in dopamine lit up, the same areas activated by addiction. The findings weren't trivial. They suggested that love is not just a fleeting feeling but a profound, neurologically embedded state of being. Love, in essence, changes us.

And then there's Paul Zak, affectionately known as "Dr. Love" for his studies on oxytocin. In one study, Zak found that when people received a simple act of kindness, like a small gift or a hug, their oxytocin levels rose, and they were more likely to reciprocate with generosity and trust. It was proof that love begets love, chemically and behaviorally. One loving act can create a ripple effect of grace in the human body.

From a Christian lens, this is breathtaking. These very chemicals mirror the fruit of the Spirit described in Galatians 5:22–23: *"Love, joy, peace, patience, kindness, goodness, faithfulness, gentleness, and self-control."* Could it be that God, in His intricate design of our biology, hardwired us to reflect His love through our very bodies?

When we love, our brains align with divine design. When we connect, forgive, and nurture, we echo the fingerprints of our Creator.

Science tells us what scripture has always whispered to the soul: love is healing.

One of the most powerful examples comes from the Harvard Study of Adult Development, which began in 1938 and is still ongoing today. Researchers have followed hundreds of individuals over their entire lives, trying to understand what makes people happy and healthy. The results? It wasn't money. It wasn't success. It wasn't fame. The clearest predictor of long-term well-being was the quality of close relationships, in other words, the presence of love.

Love doesn't just make life meaningful. It literally sustains it.

People who feel deeply loved and supported tend to:

- Have lower cortisol levels, meaning they experience less toxic stress.

- Heal from injuries more quickly. In a UCLA study, married couples who showed warmth and empathy toward one another healed faster from small wounds than those who showed tension or hostility.

- Live longer. Multiple studies have found that individuals who are socially connected and emotionally supported have lower mortality rates and are less likely to suffer from chronic illness.

In every cell of our being, love strengthens us. It boosts our immune system, balances our hormones, and enhances our resilience. Where bitterness and loneliness corrode the body over time, love nourishes and protects it.

This truth is captured beautifully in Proverbs 17:22: *"A merry heart does good like medicine."* This ancient wisdom isn't just poetic, it's scientific. Joy and connection are as essential to human health as water and sunlight.

When we experience love, our hearts beat slower. Our blood pressure stabilizes. Our minds become clearer. And our spirits rise. It's as though God placed in our biology a secret: that the way to live well is not through power or performance, but through love, given and received freely.

II. Psychological Effects

We tend to think of love as a feeling that simply happens to us. It's a spark, a comfort, a connection. But love, especially when consistent and nurtured, is far more than a fleeting emotion. It becomes the scaffolding upon which we build our identity, morality, and sense of purpose. Love isn't just about how we feel, it's about who we become.

From our very first breath, love, or the absence of it, begins shaping the architecture of our minds. The human psyche is remarkably sensitive to connection. The earliest moments of being seen, soothed, and held do not vanish with time, they lay the foundation for how we regulate our emotions, relate to others, and understand ourselves.

And throughout life, love continues to act as a powerful agent of change, challenging us to grow beyond our selfish instincts, to care for others, and to anchor our values in something deeper than survival.

Psychologists John Bowlby and Mary Ainsworth revolutionized our understanding of early childhood development with what became known as Attachment Theory, a body of research from the 1950s through the 1970s that continues to inform everything from parenting to therapy today.

At its core, Attachment Theory suggests that the way a child bonds with their caregiver, whether securely, anxiously, avoidantly, or disorganized, shapes how that child will later navigate emotional life. When a caregiver responds consistently with warmth, affection, and presence, the child learns that the world is safe and that their needs matter. This leads to what psychologists call a secure attachment, the gold standard for emotional health.

Children with secure attachments grow up more likely to form trusting relationships, manage stress, and handle conflict without falling apart. They are also more likely to develop a stable sense of identity, grounded in the assurance that they are loved, regardless of their performance.

But when love is inconsistent, cold, or withheld entirely, it leaves deep psychological scars. The child may grow up anxious, constantly seeking approval. Or detached, avoiding intimacy to protect themselves. In both cases, the absence of love doesn't just hurt, it distorts who we are.

And yet, isn't that the echo of something much deeper? The Christian understanding of God's love paints a picture of the perfect parent, a God who sees us, pursues us, and never abandons us, no matter how often we run. This is beautifully illustrated in Luke 15, the Parable of the Prodigal Son. Here we see not just a father, but a figure of divine love who waits on the horizon, arms open, ready to restore identity and dignity to the child who has lost his way.

In many ways, the story reflects what modern psychology has only recently come to understand: love not only comforts, it restores. A securely loved child becomes a whole person. A securely loved adult learns to give that same security to others.

But love does more than stabilize us emotionally. It challenges us morally. It invites us to look beyond ourselves, to consider the pain, dignity, and humanity of others. This moral movement from "me" to "we" is one of the most profound transformations love can bring.

Psychologist C. Daniel Batson explored this in his Empathy-Altruism Hypothesis during the 1980s. In a series of experiments, Batson tested whether people were motivated to help others purely out of self-interest or whether love-driven empathy could lead to genuine altruism, even when no reward was expected. He found that when people felt empathetic connection to someone in distress, they were far more likely to help, even at personal cost.

This suggested something revolutionary: that love doesn't just lead to niceness. It leads to sacrificial goodness. It fuels the kind of help that expects nothing in return.

Another powerful study, the Good Samaritan Experiment (1973), was conducted by social psychologists John Darley and Daniel Batson. Inspired by the biblical parable, they wanted to see if seminary students would stop to help a man slumped over in apparent distress. Interestingly, the variable that made the biggest difference wasn't personality, it was whether the students were in a hurry. But even more importantly, when they had just been reminded of the Parable of the Good Samaritan, they were far more likely to stop and help.

This tells us something profound. When love, and specifically faith-based love, is made conscious, we behave differently. We become different.

Jesus' words in Mark 12:31, *"Love your neighbor as yourself,"* were not abstract advice. They were a call to action. A roadmap for how to live in the world. And science is catching up with that wisdom. Studies show that individuals who regularly engage in religious reflection or spiritual practice that centers on compassion are more likely to engage in prosocial behaviors, helping, giving, forgiving.

And perhaps that makes sense. When we are immersed in a faith that teaches us that we are all beloved creations of God, we start seeing others differently. Not as strangers, but as brothers. Not as burdens, but as sacred.

Love holds a mirror to our deepest selves. It shows us who we are, not just who we pretend to be. It draws out our capacity for patience, for mercy, for hope. But it also shatters false mirrors. It interrupts the lies we've absorbed: that we are alone, unworthy, or unlovable.

In therapy rooms around the world, people heal not simply through techniques, but through attunement, the loving presence of another who listens without judgment. In marriages that flourish, it's not perfection that holds them together, but the daily act of choosing love again. In friendships that last, it's the grace to be vulnerable without fear.

And in every one of these, the pattern is the same: love transforms us. It steadies our emotions, reshapes our identities, and pulls us outward into a life of moral meaning.

From Bowlby's infants to Batson's altruists, from scripture to science, the message resounds: love grows us. It disciplines, softens, molds, and empowers. And when that love is rooted in faith, in the belief that we are loved by a God who never lets go, it becomes not only a catalyst for growth, but for redemption.

Love, in this light, is not weak or naive. It is the most serious, transformative force we will ever encounter.

III. Social Transformation

We speak of love so casually, as if it were some faint perfume that lingers in passing, something found in a glance, in a tender whisper, a folded letter forgotten in a drawer. And yes, it is those things, it is. But it is also known that one can be tormented by the conviction that love, true love, cannot remain folded and tucked away like some precious relic. It refuses to be still. It grows restless. It burns.

Love does not stay confined to the gentle corners of the heart. No. It bursts through walls. It refuses secrecy. It will not be content with mere sentiment. It becomes action. It becomes sacrifice. It steps out into the street and confronts the world, wild-eyed and trembling. It embraces the stranger, it takes the side of the weak, and it dares to interrupt the ordinary.

At first, love was considered to be something soft, something private. But love, when it is pure, when it is drenched in suffering and truth, it becomes violent in the most holy way. It upends injustice, rends the veil of indifference, and demands that we *see* one another. Not as objects. Not as obstacles. But as sacred beings: wounded, yearning, beloved.

And tell me, how can a man claim to love and walk past the beggar? How can a woman kneel in prayer, whispering "God is love," and yet despise her neighbor's sorrow? No, no, it is not love unless it does something, unless it wounds us first with compassion and then drives us mad with the desire to act.

Love tends to bind together what violence has scattered; love tends to shame the clever cynic into silence; love tends to transform even the hardened convict in his cell. I have seen love make saints out of the most miserable of men, and cowards out of the proud.

Love does not hide behind locked doors. That is not love, but comfort. And comfort is the great deceiver. Love, when it is true, comes with fire. And fire consumes. But oh, how beautifully it illuminates.

In every era, from early Christian communities to the civil rights marches of the 20th century, love has proven itself to be more than a sentiment. It is a radical force that transforms not only individuals, but entire cultures. Today, research confirms what the early Church embodied: love, when practiced in community, becomes a powerful engine of cohesion, resilience, and healing.

Human beings are not meant to live in isolation. We are wired for connection. And the presence or absence of love in our social environments can mean the difference between wholeness and fragmentation.

In recent decades, sociologists and psychologists have turned their attention to intentional religious communities like Bruderhof and L'Arche, groups that structure their lives around faith, service, and communal love. These communities are not perfect, but they offer a living example of what it means to build a social order on love rather than competition.

A 2015 study published in the *Journal of Religion and Health* found that members of such communities consistently reported higher levels of trust, forgiveness, life satisfaction, and emotional well-being compared to those in more individualistic societies. In L'Arche communities, where people with and without intellectual disabilities live together in mutual care, love becomes a great equalizer. Every member is seen as worthy, not for what they contribute economically, but simply for who they are.

Love, in these settings, is not abstract, it's embodied. It shows up in cooking meals together, in offering grace during conflict, in gathering for worship as a daily rhythm. What researchers observe in these communities is a deep psychological truth: when people know they are loved and needed, they thrive.

This echoes the early Christian model in Acts 2:42–47, where believers lived with "glad and sincere hearts," sharing everything, breaking bread together, and lifting each other in prayer. These first gatherings weren't just about worship, they were about forming a new kind of society, one that rejected status, greed, and exclusion in favor of belonging, sacrifice, and radical hospitality.

Love, when practiced communally, becomes a structure, not just a feeling. It creates safety where there was fear. Justice where there was inequality. And beauty where there was brokenness.

But the power of love doesn't stop within cloistered communities. Throughout history, love has moved into the streets. It has resisted evil, protected the vulnerable, and shifted the course of nations. It is not sentimental, it is revolutionary.

One of the most haunting and inspiring examples comes from the era of World War II, during the Holocaust. Thousands of Jewish children were hidden by courageous non-Jewish families across Europe, often at great personal risk. These "Hidden Children," as they came to be known, were studied years later by psychologists and historians seeking to understand what factors helped some survivors rebuild their lives.

The findings were striking: children who experienced consistent love and nurturing from their rescuers, even if separated from biological family, were more resilient, more emotionally stable, and more trusting of others in adulthood. In contrast, children who were hidden but emotionally neglected or mistreated often suffered long-term psychological consequences.

This wasn't just about safety, it was about the quality of love received during crisis. Love, even when delivered by strangers, had a healing power stronger than trauma. As one survivor put it, "I lost my parents, but I gained someone who made me believe the world could still be good."

Fast forward two decades to the American Civil Rights Movement, and we see love once again at the heart of profound societal change. Dr. Martin Luther King Jr., a Christian minister and visionary leader, didn't just advocate for political equality, he preached the gospel of agape love. This wasn't soft tolerance or shallow kindness. Agape was, to him, "understanding, redeeming good will for all men." It was the active, courageous choice to love one's enemies and respond to hatred with dignity and truth.

The movement's marches, sit-ins, and speeches were not driven by rage alone, they were fueled by a deep moral and theological conviction: that love could transform even the most entrenched injustice. And it did. Though the struggle was long and costly, the Civil Rights Movement reshaped laws, challenged consciences, and revealed the moral poverty of a system built on division.

Recent neuroscientific studies give us a glimpse of why love, especially in community, is so powerful. In a 2016 study by researchers at Oxford, scientists used brain imaging to study people engaged in collective worship and singing. They found that group rituals, particularly those involving synchronized movement or sound, synchronized brainwaves and elevated pain thresholds, creating a feeling of unity and euphoria.

This effect, sometimes called "neural synchrony," suggests that shared spiritual experiences literally bring people into alignment. When we worship together, sing together, or serve together, we don't just feel close, we become biologically attuned to one another. Our brains and bodies align with love's rhythm.

In Christian theology, this has always been known intuitively. When Jesus said, *"Where two or three are gathered in my name, there am I among them"* (Matthew 18:20), He pointed to something beyond symbolism. Love doesn't just bring people together, it fuses them into something more.

Love, when it becomes more than a private feeling and enters the kingdom of social policy and public life, has measurable effects on entire communities. Consider restorative justice programs, which prioritize healing relationships over punishment. Or trauma-informed schools that understand misbehavior as a cry for connection. Or churches that provide safe harbor for the homeless, the grieving, and the outcast.

In each case, love shifts the question from *"What is wrong with you?"* to *"What happened to you, and how can we walk with you toward healing?"* That shift is not just psychological. It is spiritual. It is profoundly Christlike.

If love can change brains, bodies, and behavior, if it can rebuild children, ignite movements, and bind strangers into family, then what might it do for our fractured world?

The evidence is before us. Love fosters resilience in the face of terror. It creates unity in places of division. It heals where nothing else has worked. And always, it demands action.

The first believers didn't just preach love, they structured their lives around it. The rescuers during WWII didn't just feel sympathy, they risked everything. The civil rights activists didn't just hope for justice, they walked into fire holding onto the belief that love was stronger than hate.

That is the calling still before us. To let love move from the heart to the hands. From belief to behavior. From the private to the public.

Because love, when truly lived, is not weak. It is the most powerful social force the world has ever known.

195

IV. Love, Faith, and Personal Transformation

Love is not only a balm to the hurting or a glue for relationships. It is also a force of profound transformation. When we are truly loved, when we feel seen, forgiven, and accepted at our most broken, something changes within us. Not just emotionally, but physically. Spiritually. Neurobiologically. Love rewires us.

The Christian tradition has long spoken of being "born again" a total renewal of the self that occurs not through performance, effort, or moral perfection, but through the acceptance of divine love. And now, neuroscience is beginning to affirm what faith has claimed for millennia: transformation is real, and love is its catalyst.

Dr. Andrew Newberg, a pioneer in the field of neurotheology, has spent decades studying how spiritual experiences affect the brain. Using advanced brain imaging technologies like SPECT and fMRI, he has scanned the brains of monks, nuns, Pentecostal Christians, and even atheists who underwent powerful spiritual awakenings.

What he found is astonishing: during moments of deep prayer, worship, or spiritual surrender, specific regions of the brain light up, particularly the frontal lobes (responsible for focus and intentionality) and the parietal lobes (involved in sense of self). In intense spiritual states, activity in the parietal lobes decreases, often correlating with a feeling of ego-dissolution or union with something greater. In other words, people report losing their small, isolated sense of self and experiencing oneness with God, and their brain reflects this shift.

This neurological transformation isn't just momentary. Newberg's studies suggest that long-term spiritual practice, especially when grounded in love, forgiveness, and connection, can lead to lasting changes in the brain: less anxiety, more empathy, greater emotional regulation.

A conversion experience, then, isn't just an emotional high. It is often the gateway to a deep rewiring of perception, identity, and behavior.

But perhaps more powerful than the brain scans are the stories, countless testimonies of people whose lives have been utterly upended by love. And not just any love, Christ-centered love.

Take the story of Darryl Burton, a man wrongfully imprisoned for over 24 years for a crime he didn't commit. In prison, Darryl was filled with bitterness, rage, and hopelessness, until, one day, he came across a verse from the Gospel of Luke: *"Father, forgive them, for they know not what they do."* He was stunned. How could Jesus offer forgiveness in the face of cruelty? That moment planted a seed that would grow into faith. Darryl came to Christ in prison, and the bitterness that had poisoned him for decades began to fade. He now runs a ministry for the incarcerated and speaks about the transformative power of love that reached him in his darkest place.

Similarly, in programs like Teen Challenge, a Christian recovery ministry for addicts, thousands of former drug users testify that what years of therapy and punishment couldn't do, love did. Not condemnation. Not control. But the overwhelming, undeserved love of God. Love that says: *You are not your past. You are mine.*

Science supports what these stories proclaim. Studies on religious conversion among inmates and addicts show significant decreases in recidivism, drug use, and violent behavior, often because these individuals begin to see themselves as beloved, forgiven, and valuable.

As Paul writes in 2 Corinthians 5:17, *"If anyone is in Christ, he is a new creation; the old has gone, the new has come."* This is not metaphor, it is psychological, neurological, and existential truth. When we are touched by love that does not condemn but redeems, we begin to walk differently. Think differently. Love differently.

If love transforms, then forgiveness is its purest form. To forgive is not to forget or excuse. It is to choose love over vengeance, to release the chains of bitterness and reclaim peace.

Psychologist Dr. Robert Enright, often called the father of forgiveness research, developed a structured therapeutic approach known as Forgiveness Therapy. His studies, particularly among victims of abuse, trauma survivors, and those suffering from deep betrayal, revealed that people who learned to forgive through a step-by-step process experienced reduced depression, anxiety, and anger, as well as improved physical health.

In one study, individuals who participated in forgiveness interventions showed greater emotional healing than those who pursued other cognitive therapies. Why? Because forgiveness does something deeper. It touches the soul.

Neuroscience offers further support. A 2014 study using fMRI found that when people genuinely forgave someone who hurt them, the limbic system (associated with pain and anger) calmed down, and areas related to empathy and moral reasoning lit up. The very act of forgiving brings the brain back to balance. It helps us reprocess pain not with fear, but with grace.

Christianity, of course, places forgiveness at the center of its message. *"Love keeps no record of wrongs"* (1 Corinthians 13:5).

Jesus does not just preach forgiveness, He embodies it. At the height of His own suffering, He cries out for mercy for His killers. In doing so, He models for us the most radical form of love: redemptive love.

Forgiveness in the Christian framework is not about minimizing harm. It is about healing hearts. It allows victims to stop drinking the poison of resentment and to start walking in freedom. And for those who have caused harm, divine forgiveness offers something even more shocking: the chance to begin again.

Redemption is the thread that runs through every Christian testimony, every revival, every changed life. Love that is patient, kind, and keeps no record of wrongs. Love that rebuilds what shame and sin tore down. Love that doesn't just renovate, it resurrects.

If love has the power to transform, then what happens when it is withheld? When warmth, connection, and affection are absent, not just occasionally, but persistently?

Science offers a sobering answer: without love, we do not flourish. We fracture.

In the 1950s, psychologist Harry Harlow conducted one of the most famous, and ethically troubling, experiments in the study of attachment. He took infant rhesus monkeys and separated them from their mothers, offering them instead two surrogate "mothers": one made of wire that dispensed milk, and one covered in soft cloth but offering no food.

To the researchers' surprise, the monkeys consistently clung to the cloth mother, even when the wire mother provided nourishment. Comfort, not sustenance, was their priority. And the longer they were deprived of real maternal care, the more psychologically disturbed they became, rocking back and forth, showing signs of depression, aggression, and severe social deficits.

The conclusion was heartbreaking and clear: love is not optional. It is as necessary as food and water.

Decades later, a more tragic human version of this played out in the Romanian orphanages following the fall of dictator Nicolae Ceaușescu. Tens of thousands of children had been raised in institutional neglect, fed and clothed, but starved of affection, eye contact, or consistent caregivers.

When researchers from Harvard and other institutions studied these children, the findings were alarming: severe developmental delays, attachment disorders, emotional flatness, and in many cases, permanent damage to the brain's emotional and cognitive centers.

MRI scans of these children revealed smaller brain volume, particularly in areas tied to emotion regulation and executive functioning. Even years after being adopted into loving homes, many of them struggled to form trust or to process empathy.

These children weren't broken because of trauma alone. They were broken by the absence of love, a lack of holding, smiling, soothing, and the daily rhythms of human connection.

Scripture speaks to this truth with painful clarity. In 1 Corinthians 13:1–2, Paul writes:

"If I speak in the tongues of men and of angels, but have not love, I am a noisy gong or a clanging cymbal... If I have all faith, so as to move mountains, but have not love, I am nothing."

This is more than poetic language. It is spiritual neuroscience. You can have all the talent, intelligence, and faith in the world, but without love, the soul begins to hollow. Without love, nothing truly grows. We become, as Paul says, nothing.

Modern psychology now confirms this in chilling terms: emotional neglect can be more damaging than physical harm. To be unloved is to be unseen, and the human spirit cannot survive for long when invisible.

What emerges from both scripture and science is a single, unshakable truth: we were made for love. Not for performance. Not for perfection. But for love.

When we are loved, we become fully alive. When we are unloved, we begin to disappear, from others, from God, even from ourselves.

And the miracle of faith is that no matter how deep our wounds, how long our loneliness, or how hardened our hearts, love is still possible. In Christ, the love we never received can be found. The love we withheld can be forgiven. The love we long for can be lived.

Because love doesn't just come from us, it comes through us, from the One who *is* love.

V. Divine Love

In every study, every brain scan, every personal story, one truth keeps rising to the surface: love changes us. It rewires our neural pathways, repairs emotional fractures, reshapes relationships, and redirects entire communities. But as beautiful and potent as human love is, there is a love that goes even deeper. A love not born of hormones, chance, or cultural rituals. A love that is not earned, not diminished by failure, and not undone by death.

That love is Divine Love, what Christians call agape. It is not simply the best kind of love. It is love's very source.

In his profound work *The Four Loves*, C.S. Lewis lays out the hierarchy of love: *storge* (affection), *philia* (friendship), *eros* (romantic love), and finally, *agape*, selfless, divine love. Unlike the other loves, which arise naturally and often self-servingly, agape is a love that chooses, regardless of what is returned. It is the love that *gives anyway*. It is the love that bears all things, believes all things, hopes all things, endures all things.

Lewis described agape as the love God shows us, and the love He invites us to extend to others. Not because they deserve it, but because that is the kind of love that restores the world.

N.T. Wright, one of today's leading biblical scholars, takes this further. In his vision of Christian eschatology, he writes that love is not only God's nature, it is God's future. Wright sees love as the very engine of new creation, the force through which God is renewing heaven and earth. Every act of agape is not just a moral good, it is a participation in the redemption of the world.

So, when a mother forgives the person who killed her son.

When an addict chooses the long, hard path of sobriety because someone believed in them.

When a man on death row discovers that he is more than his worst mistake.

These are not just emotional triumphs. They are glimpses of resurrection. Echoes of eternal love made manifest in time.

If agape love transforms the world, it first transforms the soul. History is filled with men and women who were utterly changed by divine love, and whose lives, in turn, became beacons for others.

St. Teresa of Ávila, a 16th-century mystic, once wrote of her experiences with God's love as "a wound so sweet it both burns and heals." She described her suffering, both physical and spiritual, not as meaningless torment, but as the fire through which her soul was refined. Love, she said, was not an escape from pain. It was the transformation of pain into purpose.

Similarly, Julian of Norwich, a medieval anchoress who lived through the Black Death and personal isolation, penned one of the most hopeful visions of God's love in all of Christian literature: *"All shall be well, and all shall be well, and all manner of thing shall be well."* These words weren't written in a time of peace, but in the wake of catastrophic suffering. And yet, through divine love, Julian glimpsed a reality deeper than despair. A love that holds even history's darkest chapters in its embrace.

Their insights are not relics of the past. Today, countless people walk through trauma, illness, grief, and loss, and find, in the depths, not a void, but a presence. A still small voice that says, *You are loved. You are not alone.*

Every field of study, every branch of human knowledge, is converging on the same truth: we were made for love. Love is not a soft sentiment. It is the most powerful force in the universe. And when that love originates not just from within us, but from beyond us, from the heart of God, it becomes the very thing that makes us new.

This is why Christian love is so radical. It does not wait for worthiness. It does not require reciprocation. It does not operate by fairness. It offers grace when we expect judgment. It gives wholeness in exchange for brokenness. And in doing so, it reveals to us who we truly are: image-bearers of the God who is love (1 John 4:8).

Love isn't something we stumbled into as a species. It's not an evolutionary glitch or cultural invention. Love, especially agape love, is woven into the very structure of creation. And when we lean into it, scientifically, emotionally, spiritually, we begin to experience life as it was meant to be.

You see, there is a moment, now distant but never diminished, that etched itself into the marrow of my memory, a moment when love, in all its intangible glory, became undeniably physical.

I was poring over a study, quiet and largely forgotten in the folds of early 21st-century research. It emerged from the institutional walls of Russian orphanages, where infants were fed, changed, clothed, their physical survival assured. And yet, those rooms were not filled with life, but with silence. Sterile, efficient silence.

The kind of silence that bruises the soul.

You see, these children had everything except the one thing they needed most: love. Not sentiment. Not metaphor. But the embodied, responsive presence of another. Touch, when it came, was procedural. Smiles were measured. Voices spoke only in necessity. And in those bare nurseries, one could witness a truth both tragic and clinical: a baby would cry, and no one came. Over time, the crying ceased. Not out of peace, but because the body, in its tragic genius, adapts. The soul, still divine, learns to become silent in a world that will not answer.

Reading this, my heart broke, not only for the children confined within those pale rooms, but for the child within myself who once believed that quiet endurance was the same as safety.

But what that research uncovered was more than sadness. It revealed something sacred. That love is not a luxury of poets

204

or theologians, it is a biological imperative. It is a neurological necessity. It is spiritual oxygen.

Children who received warm, consistent care, whose needs were met not just with competence but with kindness, those children began to thrive. Their brains formed faster. Their immune systems grew stronger. Their joy returned like spring to a frostbitten land. Meanwhile, those deprived of that essential human warmth often remained smaller, spoke later, and carried the imprint of neglect long after they were removed from the setting, even after adoption, even into adulthood.

It was here that the veil between science and faith fell away for me. I began to see with clarity: Love is how the brain wires. Love is how the body heals. Love is how the spirit remembers it is alive.

And as I wept, not just academically, but personally, I returned, as I always do, to the Scriptures.

"The Lord is close to the brokenhearted and saves those who are crushed in spirit." (Psalm 34:18)

I believe this verse not as an abstract comfort, but as a scientific affirmation. Because love saves, not only souls but cells. Not only eternities but nervous systems. The rhythm of a mother's voice, the warmth of an attentive gaze, the soothing cadence of being seen, these are not emotional accessories. These are foundations of humanity.

In the laws of energy, emotion is motion. And when love flows, life flourishes. When withheld, growth slows, resilience weakens, and something elemental dims. This is not just a theory. It is observable. Measurable. Universal.

And yet, where data falters, grace continues.

Because I have seen miracles. The kind no chart can capture. Adults, once fractured by abandonment, who became the most devoted nurturers of others. Generational trauma interrupted by one praying grandmother or a father who chose tenderness over tradition. I've witnessed the impossible become inevitable when love, stubborn, holy love, enters the room.

This is what I write of. This harmony between neurons and Spirit. Between divine order and the mess of human experience. A melody written long before we knew what dopamine was, and sung still by the God who shaped the limbic system with His own breath.

So, if you've ever felt forgotten, like those infants in quiet cribs, if your wounds are invisible but persistent, know this:

You were seen.

You are seen.

And even your silence was heard.

Because God does not require language to understand anguish. And even the unanswered cries of your soul are seeds, seeds planted in the soil of divine redemption, destined to bloom in His time.

This book you hold is born of that revelation. It is the cry that found its voice. The data that met the divine. The story of love, told through broken systems and holy whispers.

So here's the final question, the question that hums behind every scientific finding and theological claim: If love can change our brains, heal our bodies, repair our relationships, and restore our communities... what can the love of God do?

The answer isn't theoretical. It's personal.

It can make addicts sober.

It can soften enemies into friends.

It can turn despair into courage, hatred into mercy, ashes into beauty.

It can make old things new.

It can make dead things live.

And it can begin in you. Right now. Because, as Scripture promises:

"We love because He first loved us."

— 1 John 4:19

This is where science and faith meet. At the foot of love.

Not a love we earn.

Not a love we create.

But a love that creates us.

Reflective Questions

When you think of love, do you think of comfort or confrontation? Have you ever experienced a love that disturbed your peace and challenged your worldview?

_____

_____

_____

_____

Do you believe that love, if lived fully, can reshape entire communities, or even societies? If so, what keeps you from loving that way in your own life?

_____

_____

_____

_____

What kind of love do you find easier to give, love that comforts or love that corrects, disrupts, restores? Why do you think that is?

_____

_____

_____

When have you withheld love out of fear, pride, or fatigue? What would it look like to return to that moment now, with grace?

_____

_____

_____

_____

Have you ever witnessed love transform a person, perhaps even yourself, in ways logic or reason could not explain? What power was at work in that transformation?

_____

_____

_____

_____

When you look at the world today, where do you see love disrupting injustice, restoring dignity, or binding wounds? Are you participating in that kind of love, or only admiring it from afar?

_____

_____

_____

If God is love, and love is action, what is He asking you to do with your love? Not someday, not ideally, but now?

_____

_____

_____

_____

Conclusion

There was a time, though it feels less like time and more like eternity compressed into skin, when I awoke each day inside a body I no longer recognized. My limbs obeyed gravity but disobeyed peace. My skin felt too thin, as if the air itself bruised me. There was no wound to bandage, no diagnosis to chase. Only pain, feral, untamed, moving through me like a storm with no map.

From the outside, I appeared fine. I smiled. I answered questions. I stood upright in rooms full of people. But inside… inside I was drowning. Every nerve was fire. Every breath, a weight. There were days I forgot what it meant to be clear-headed. Other days, I forgot what it meant not to weep.

Doctors, kind but confused, handed me sterile terms and silent pills. Some suggested depression. Others whispered psychosomatic. The worst looked at me with pity. None looked at me with understanding. And yet I knew. I knew what they couldn't name. Something ancient and aching was lodged in my bones. Something deeper than illness. Something sacred.

They called it fibromyalgia, eventually. A mouthful of consonants that tried to describe a disorder of the nervous system, a hypersensitive brain that turns whispers into alarms. Science calls it central sensitization. But long before I found the words, I knew it in the language of suffering. The body was crying out because the soul had been silent for too long.

"My flesh and my heart may fail, but God is the strength of my heart and my portion forever."

—Psalm 73:26

So I began to ask…not just "What is this?" but Why? Not just "How do I stop it?" but What is it trying to teach me?

The answers didn't come from textbooks, but from the hush of prayer and the hum of memory. I read studies on the HPA axis, the body's stress system, and saw how trauma reconfigures biology. I learned that prolonged grief, suppressed anger, unspoken fear, these things reroute the flow of hormones, corrode the rhythm of sleep, inflame the nervous system. Pain, then, was not just punishment. It was a sacred alarm bell.

And I saw, in that, the fingerprints of divine design.

"For we are fearfully and wonderfully made; your works are wonderful, I know that full well."

—Psalm 139:14

I realized my pain wasn't random. It was truth trying to surface. Years of overextending. Years of saying "yes" when I meant "no." Years of swallowing emotion for the sake of being likable, useful, quiet. My body was the archivist of unloved moments. Every ache was an unopened letter. Every flare of pain, a sermon I hadn't heard.

"The spirit of a man will sustain him in sickness, but who can bear a broken   spirit?"
—Proverbs 18:14

But healing didn't begin in the clinic. It began in the dark.

Fibromyalgia, they say, is "invisible." But it is not. It's the visible expression of hidden sorrow. It is a ghost-pain, yes, but the ghosts are real. They are old versions of ourselves we've long buried. But grace exhumes them not to condemn, but to redeem.

So let me say this to you now, if you are the one waking in the dark. If you are the one whose body whispers in pain what your lips cannot say:

You are not weak. You are not forgotten. You are not broken beyond repair. Your pain is not your enemy, it may be your unspoken truth. It may be the sacred language your body uses when your soul has grown too tired to speak.

And know this: God sees it. He felt the nails in His own body so He could understand yours. The same God who created the laws of neurology walks with you through every flare, every fog, every fatigue.

"Now may the God of peace Himself sanctify you completely; and may your whole spirit, soul, and body be preserved blameless..."

—1 Thessalonians 5:23

It began at 3:00 a.m. when the world was asleep and pain would not let me join them. I lay there, not just aching in body, but raw in spirit, and I began to pray. Not elegant prayers. Not polished ones. Just honest ones. Prayers that spilled out like broken water jars.

I didn't pray for escape. I prayed for meaning. I didn't ask, "Why me?" I asked, "What now?" And in the stillness, when I stopped pleading and started listening, I heard it, not audibly, but undeniably:

You are not being punished. You are being purified.

That one sentence undid years of self-condemnation. It untied the knots in my nervous system. It whispered to the tightness in my chest: Peace is not the absence of symptoms, it's the presence of trust.

And something began to shift. Not overnight. But over time.

213

"He heals the brokenhearted and binds up their wounds."

—Psalm 147:3

Science gave me language. But faith gave me resurrection.

Neuroplasticity taught me that the brain can be rewired. And Scripture told me that the mind can be renewed. Forgiveness, gratitude, prayer, they don't just lift the soul. They reconfigure the circuitry of the brain. Each act of love becomes a thread of healing. Each whispered prayer becomes a balm to cells starved for safety.

"Do not conform to the pattern of this world, but be transformed by the renewing of your mind."

—Romans 12:2

So I laid hands on myself and read the Psalms out loud. I sang when my voice cracked. I cried in worship and let the tears baptize the sorrow that words could not reach. I stopped asking for perfection and started reaching for presence.

God did not remove the storm, but He anchored me inside it.

There is a holy harmony that science alone cannot explain: pain met purpose, diagnosis met design, and I met my Healer not in absence of pain, but through it.

There was also a moment, in the year 2004, when I lost a part of my body, a part that had grown silent, defiant, immovable. My colon was removed, carved out like a forgotten corridor of myself after a diagnosis they called Colonic Inertia, and later, almost mockingly, Gastroparesis. But long before medicine renamed it, I had already felt its tyranny.

Inertia.

The word clung to me like a second skin. It wasn't just a description of my gut, it was a portrait of my existence. I was not merely ill. I was stuck. Trapped in a body that would not move, inside a spirit that dared not speak, inside a life that had folded in on itself.

I was static.

No forward. No fire. No voice. Just the slow suffocation of stillness.

But even Newton, Newton! whispers through the corridors of science and Scripture alike: *A body in motion stays in motion... unless acted upon by an outside force.*

And God, yes, God, was my outside force.

Not a thunderclap. Not a flood. He didn't tear down the door with fury. No. He entered softly, like breath at the edge of sleep. Like light through closed eyelids. He did not scream me back to life. He spoke me back to it.

Not with violence, but with mercy. Not with noise, but with truth. He interrupted my inertia with grace.

And in that divine interruption, something began again, not just in my body, but in the architecture of my soul. The motion that sickness had stolen was not lost; it was suspended. Waiting. And God, in His unfathomable kindness, unfroze me.

He whispered to the dust of me and said, "Move again."

So here's my final word to you, my reader, if you are suffering now, physically, emotionally, or in the aching spaces where words dare not tread, hear me.

You are not abandoned. You are being awakened.

Even if your limbs fail you, even if your heart aches from carrying what no one else sees, even if you cannot remember what it felt like to be whole, you are still being led.

Your healing may not look like lightning. It may come like dew: soft, unnoticed, and absolutely real. Even now, something inside you is shifting. The Spirit is brooding over the chaos. The Author is turning the page.

Science is not the enemy of faith. It is its echo. Its language. Its scaffolding. And prayer is not a wish, it is a resurrection seed. It is the breath that speaks to dead places and says, *Live*.

You do not have to choose between faith and facts. You only have to trust that the God who wrote the laws of motion also knows how to move the immovable within you.

And He is not finished. Not with your body. Not with your mind. Not with your story.

He is still writing. And there are pages yet to turn.

Because I know… there was a time, perhaps in all of us, when I feared that loving God meant forsaking reason. That faith and science were opponents in some ancient, invisible war, each demanding my loyalty while tearing at different halves of my soul. I thought belief required the blindfolding of intellect, and that devotion was incompatible with inquiry. But slowly, painfully, beautifully, I have come to realize: truth has never been divided. Only our perception of it has.

I have studied science, not as a skeptic, but as a seeker. I have gazed into the mysteries of cell division, the spiral staircase of DNA, the laws that govern black holes and neurons alike. I've read the research, held the microscope, stared at brain scans glowing with electric pulses of thought and memory, emotion and awe. And what did I find there, deep in the heart of logic, structure, and measurable law? Not emptiness. Not randomness. Not cold detachment.

I found design. I found intelligence. I found God.

With every chart I studied and every structure I marveled at, I moved not further from the divine, but closer, closer than I had ever dared believe. Because what is science if not the language of God's architecture? What are the laws of nature if not the reflection of a lawgiver? The atoms, the galaxies, the tides, the seasons, they do not speak chaos. They whisper a rhythm. A pattern. A sacred precision that echoes Genesis: *"And God saw that it was good."*

The universe does not behave like an accident. It behaves like a thought that has never stopped unfolding. The more I explored, the more I discovered that the Bible had never been in conflict with reality. It had always been *ahead* of it. Faith didn't crumble under the weight of scientific truth, it stood up straighter, clearer, stronger, its foundation deeper than I imagined.

"World without end. Amen." —Ephesians 3:21.

Those words are not just poetic. They are astrophysical. They speak to an eternal unfolding, a cosmos that expands without apology, just as love does. Just as grace does. "World without end" is not merely benediction, it is the declaration of a universe sustained by more than energy. Sustained by intention. By God's wisdom.

We have been sold a false tension: that faith is primitive and science is progress. But in truth, they do not oppose, they complete. Faith asks *why*. Science shows *how*. And both, when honest, stand in reverence at the threshold of mystery and say: *this is beyond us, and yet, it is for us.*

There is no dividing wall here. There is only wonder. The microscope and the psalmist sing the same song, if only we have ears to hear it. The equations on a physicist's board, and the prayers of a shepherd king under the stars, are not rivals, they are kin. The universe is not afraid of Scripture. And Scripture is not afraid of discovery. They are reflections of the same Source.

So if you, dear reader, have ever been told that you must choose, between the sacred and the scientific, between reason and revelation, know this: you have been misled. The Creator of the atom is the same One who numbers the hairs on your head. The God who spoke galaxies into being is not offended by your questions. He invented the brain that forms them.

Faith is not the absence of thinking. It is the fullness of understanding. And science is not the absence of God, it is one of the loudest ways He speaks.

So study, question, explore. Let wonder and wisdom walk together. And know, always, that at the heart of every law, every discovery, every miracle is this unshakable truth:

The Bible was never at war with science. It was simply waiting for us to catch up.

www.ingramcontent.com/pod-product-compliance
Lightning Source LLC
Chambersburg PA
CBHW071320120626
46546CB00002B/382